Warehouse Theatre Company and **Nuffield Theatre Southampton** present

THE SHAGAROUND

a play

by **Maggie Nevill**

The Shagaround was selected from the International Playwriting Festival 1999 and was first showcased at the Warehouse Theatre in November 1999.

An Italian translation was presented at the Premio Candoni-Arta Terme festival in Italy in June 2000.

The World Premiere took place at the Nuffield Theatre, Southampton on Thursday 26 April 2001.

The first performance at Soho Theatre and Writers' Centre took place on Tuesday 24 July 2001.

Warehouse Theatre Company Regd. Charity No: 272816
Nuffield Theatre Regd. Charity No: 286876
Soho Theatre Company Regd. Charity No: 267234

THE SHAGAROUND

by **Maggie Nevill**

Sal	Elizabeth Berrington
Lisa	Luisa Bradshaw-White
Matt	Matthew Cullum
Dilly	Veronica Quilligan
Beth	Toyah Willcox
G	Diane Parish

Director	Patrick Sandford
Designer	Juliet Shillingford
Lighting Designer	David W Kidd
Assistant Director	Delia Lindsay
Fight Director	Paul Benzing

Stage Manager	Marie Costa

Production Managers:

Warehouse Theatre Co.	Graham Constable
Nuffield Theatre	Nicky Wingfield

Casting Director	Sarah Beardsall

Elizabeth Berrington, Sal

Elizabeth trained at the Webber Douglas Academy of Dramatic Art and has recently finished filming *The Grimleys*, *Sam's Game* and *The Bill*. Theatre credits include Dainty Fidget in *The Country Wife* (Sheffield Crucible), Sally Yeats in *Together* (Edinburgh Festival), Lofty in *Y A Otra Cosa Mariposa* (Battersea Arts Centre), Christine in *The Last Waltz* (Gateway Theatre, Chester), Lady Basildon in *An Ideal Husband* (Royal Exchange Theatre), Rose in *The Left-Over Heart* (Offstage Downstairs) for which she was nominated for Best Actress at the Carling Fringe Awards, Mary in *The Knocky* (Royal Court Young Writers Festival) and Clarine in *Rupert Street Lonely Hearts Club* (ETT tour, Donmar Warehouse, the Criterion) for which she was nominated for the Best Regional Theatre Awards 1996. Film credits include Charlotte in *Quills*, Elizabeth in *Little Vampires*, Pru in *Mad Cows*, Celeste in *Eight and a Half Women*, Mlle Volonsky in *Eugene Onegin*, Mrs Ash in *An Urban Ghost Story*, Giselle in *Naked* and Jane in *Secrets and Lies*. Recent television includes Mrs Robins in *The Grimleys* (Granada), Ruth in two series of *The Lakes* (BBC), three series of *My Wonderful Life* (Granada), *The Vice* (Carlton), Marie Antoinette in *Let Them Eat Cake* (Tiger Aspect for the BBC), *Nature Boy* (BBC), *Casualty* (BBC), *Silent Witness* (BBC), *The Bill* (Thames) and *Between the Lines III* (BBC).

Luisa Bradshaw-White, Lisa

Luisa is a familiar face on television, having appeared as Kira in two series of *This Life*, Lorna Rose in one series of *Bad Girls*, *London's Burning*, *Meaningful Sex*, *Active Defence*, Samantha in two series of *Big Bad World*, *Grafters*, *The Pits*, *Birds of a Feather Christmas Special*, *A Touch of Frost*, *The Bill*, *The Brittas Empire* and Maria in *Grange Hill*. Theatre work includes Lady Anne in *Richard III* (Pleasance Theatre), Kelly in *Solitary Confinement* (ICA) and Sonya in *Godspell* (Chichester Festival). Radio credits include *Under One Roof* (comedy drama series for Radio 4), *Charm Factory* (period drama for Radio 4) and *Konfidentz* (World Service). Film work includes *The Escort* (Pathe Productions), *Wonderful World* (Wiggin O'Neal Films) and *Friendship in Vienna* (Walt Disney).

Matthew Cullum, Matt

Matthew trained at the Rose Bruford College of Speech and Drama. Matthew appeared at the Nuffield in *Treasure Island*, *The Tempest*, *Wind in the Willows*, *Teechers*, *A Midsummer Night's Dream*, *The Song From the Sea*, *The Last Yellow*, *Todd's Climb* and *Thicker Than Water*. Matthew also directed last year's Shakespeare First production of *A Midsummer Night's Dream* for the Nuffield. Other theatre work includes Steven Berkoff's *Messiah* (Edinburgh Festival 2000) and Berkoff's *East* (West End,Edinburgh Festival and National no1 tour), *Into Our Dreams* (Almeida at Shoreditch Town Hall), *Hamlet* (Oxford Stage Co), *Metamorphosis* and *The Tempest* (Cheltenham Everyman), *Mickey and Me* (Worcester Swan) and *If Mr Frollo Finds Out* (Old Red Lion). Television and film work includes *Gulliver's Travels* (Jim Henson Productions), *One in a Million* (LWT) and *Our Tune* (BBC). Directing work includes Asst. on Berkoff's *East* (West End, tour), *Treats* (BAC), *The Epic of Gilgamesh* (Millennium Dome), *Gods of the Vikings* (tour) and *Animal Farm* (tour).

Diane Parish, G

Diane trained at RADA. Theatre credits include *Breath Boom* (Royal Court), Karen in *Speed the Plow* and Lulu in *The Birthday Party* (Contact Theatre, Manchester), *This is a Chair* (Royal Court), *Sweetheart* (Royal Court and tour), Leah in *Beautiful Thing* (Duke of York's), Cordelia in *King Lear* (Talawa Theatre Company), Hero in *Much Ado About Nothing* (Oxford Stage Company), *Blood Brothers*, *Yerma*, *Fuente Ovejuna*, *Romeo and Juliet*, and Minihaha in *Hiawatha* (all Bristol Old Vic), Ariel in *The Tempest* (Oxford Stage Company), and Lourdes in *An Enchanted Land* (Riverside Studios). Television includes Rachel in *Real Women* (BBC), Lisa Gee in *Picking Up The Pieces* (Carlton), Lola Christie in *Eastenders* (BBC), Donna in *Casualty* (BBC), *Holding On* (BBC), Beth in *Lovejoy* (BBC), *Complete Guide to Relationships* (Kudos), *Frank Stubbs Promotes* (Noel Gay), *Wide Eyed And Legless* (BBC), *Shakers* (BBC), Shirley in *The Vice II* (Carlton) and *Clocking Off* (Red Productions for BBC). Film work includes Millie in *The Final Passage* directed by Sir Peter Hall (Passage Productions), Millie in *Alive and Kicking* directed by Nancy Meckler (Indian Summer Films), and *Driving Miss Crazy* (Keylight Films). Diane is currently filming *Baby Father* for the BBC.

Veronica Quilligan, Dilly

Veronica's extensive theatre credits include *A Pagan Place*, *The Key Tag*, *Young Writers' Festival*, *Cove Hithe*, *From Cockney to Toffs* and *The School Leaver* all for the Royal Court, *A Lesson in Blood and Roses* (Royal Shakespeare Company), *The Way of the World*, *The Tempest*, *Spring Awakening* and Juliet in *Romeo and Juliet* (Royal National Theatre), *Salome* (RNT/Gate Theatre), Gigi in *Gigi* (Fortune Theatre, West End), *Zigomania* (Bush Theatre), *Please Shine Down on Me* (Bush Theatre/Foco Novo), *Loved* (Bush Theatre/ Tricycle), *Looking at You* (Bush Theatre/Leicester Haymarket), *The Glass Menagerie*, *Wild Oats*, *Translations* and *Says I Says He* (Bristol Old Vic), *The Country Wife* (Actors Company), *Flesh and Blood* (Triumph Apollo), *The Father* (Open Space), the lead in *Antigone* (Field Day Theatre Co. Derry), *Midnight Court* (Project Theatre, Dublin), *Faith Healer* (Traverse Theatre, Edinburgh), *Colours* (Abbey Theatre, Dublin), *Miss Julie* (Liverpool Playhouse), *Beauty and the Beast* (Liverpool Playhouse/Old Vic/West End) and *Dancing at Lughnasa* (Phoenix Garrick/West End). Television includes *Doctors* (BBC), *Rough Justice* (BBC), *Peak Practice III* (Central), *Centrepoint* (Channel 4), *Country Matters* (Granada), *Follyfoot* (YTV), *Between the Wars* (LWT), *The Wild Duck* (BBC), *Red Shift* (BBC), *Theresa* (BBC), *City Sugar* (STV), *Vanishing Army* (BBC), *The History Man* (BBC), *The Bill* (Thames) and *Tears Before Bedtime* (BBC). Films include *Call at Corazon*, *The Seaweed Children*, Ken Russell's *Listzomania*, *Robin and Marian*, *Candleshoe*, *Wildcats of St Trinian's*, Neil Jordan's *Angel*, *Hostage*, *Crime Pays*, *The Lonely Passion of Judith Hearne*, *Raggedy Rawney*, *Anchoress* and *Maria's Song*. Radio work for the BBC includes *The Street Sings*, *Winners*, *Uprooted*, *The Singular Life of Albert Nobbs*, *The Wooing of Emer*, *Pendennis*, *The Oresteia*, *Dr Barrie* and *Kitty Wilkins*.

Toyah Willcox, Beth

Toyah trained at the Old Rep Drama School in her home town of Birmingham. Her repertory theatre credits include playing Hermia in *A Midsummer Night's Dream* with Birmingham Rep, *The Choice* and *Memoirs of a Survivor* at Salisbury Playhouse, *Carrington* at Chichester Festival Theatre and most recently Beatrice in *Much Ado About Nothing* at the Ludlow Festival. In London she has twice appeared at the Royal National Theatre, playing Emma in *Tales From*

the Vienna Woods and Mary Lou in Whale. She also appeared in Sugar 'n' Spice at the Royal Court and as Puck in A Midsummer Night's Dream at the Regent's Park Open Air Theatre. In the West End she appeared in Trafford Tanzi (Mermaid Theatre), Cabaret (Strand Theatre), Three Men on a Horse (Vaudeville Theatre), American Days (ICA) and played Kate in The Taming of the Shrew (Cambridge Theatre). Toyah recently played Dora Maar in the acclaimed Picasso's Women at the Edinburgh Festival. Her television work is extensive and includes Shoestring, Dr Jekyll and Mr Hyde and Toyah – A Documentary all for the BBC. For Granada she played Gigi in Maigret and the Hotel Majestic and played opposite Laurence Olivier in the acclaimed Ebony Tower. Most recently she played the title role in two series of the BBC's Barmy Aunt Boomerang and appeared in BBC1's Doctors. On film Toyah has twice worked with Derek Jarman, as Mad in Jubilee and Miranda in The Tempest, for which she was nominated for Best Newcomer at the Evening Standard Awards. She played Monkey in Quadrophenia, played opposite Katherine Hepburn in The Corn Is Green and for the BFI she played Pauline in The Anchoress. Toyah's music career spans 13 top 40 singles and 15 solo albums, the first two of which – Sheep Farming in Barnet and Blue Meaning – became seminal to the Gothic movement. She dominated the music scene during the late '70s and early '80s, and won the Best Female Singer in the 1982 Rock and Pop Awards. This year the University of Central England awarded her an Honorary Doctorate in Media and Arts, and her autobiography Living Out Loud was released in paperback.

Patrick Sandford, Director

Patrick Sandford is the Artistic Director of the Nuffield Theatre. His London theatre work includes the modern Russian comedy Exchange by Yuri Trifonov, translated by Michael Frayn (Vaudeville Theatre); An Ideal Husband (Westminster Theatre and three national tours); In Broad Daylight (Tricycle Theatre) and The Winter Wife by Claire Tomalin, a new play about Katherine Mansfield (Lyric Theatre, Hammersmith). This production was nominated for five TMA awards. Patrick won Best Director for this and Shakespeare's Much Ado About Nothing. Abroad, his productions have been seen in South Africa, Australia, France and Germany, and he worked briefly at the Drama Theatre in Pskov, Western Russia. He was previously Artistic Director of the Lyric Theatre Belfast, and the Redgrave Theatre, Farnham. The Nuffield has presented several British premieres, notably of American and Australian plays, including Woody Allen's The Floating Light Bulb, David Williamson's Dead White Males, and most recently Tony MacNamara's comedy The John Wayne Principle, which was also seen at the Pleasance Theatre, London. Patrick recently directed The Tempest, Didier van Cauwelaert's French play Noces de Sable that received its British premiere as Beach Wedding, and last year's Christmas show, Treasure Island.

Maggie Nevill, Writer

Maggie Nevill trained at Bournemouth and Chelsea Schools of Art and subsequently embarked on an international dishwashing career before infiltrating the Nuffield Theatre front-of-house staff in 1996. Wildly inspired by Patrick Sandford's production of *Peter Pan*, she wrote a play called *Wendy Darling* which is due to be workshopped as part of the 'Feet First' season of new writing at The Yvonne Arnaud Theatre in May of this year. *The Shagaround* is Maggie's third play and was written on demand for its initial airing at a girls-only party in St. Denys. It was selected from The Warehouse Theatre's International Playwriting Festival in 1999 and performed, in Italian, at the Premio Candoni Arta Terme festival in Udine last year, under the title *Lurido Schifoso Bastardo*. Maggie would like to thank all The Wild Women of Southampton for their help and support throughout the gestation of this play. And those special men who made it happen.

Juliet Shillingford, Designer

Juliet trained at Ravensbourne and Croydon Colleges of Art, receiving a degree in Fine Art and a Diploma in Theatre Design. She was the Associate Designer for the Library Theatre, Manchester and has done freelance work for Lyric Theatre, Hammersmith and the King's Head. Recent freelance work includes *Richard III* for Leicester Haymarket and the ballet *Erte* for Bird College at the Peacock Theatre. Nuffield productions include *Rhinoceros*, *Fertility Dance*, *Sauce for the Goose*, *A Christmas Carol*, *Out of the Sun*, *Around the World in Eighty Days*, *Sly Fox*, *The Three Musketeers*, *Jungle Book*, *Robin Hood*, *Mail Order Bride*, *Peter Pan*, *Brothers of the Brush*, *Waiting for Godot*, *The Seduction of Anne Boleyn*, *Alice in Wonderland*, *Earth and Sky* and *Beach Wedding*.

David W Kidd, Lighting Designer

David is a regular contributor to the Nuffield. Previous lighting designs include *Twelfth Night*; *The Bacchae*; *Miss Julie*; *The Wind in the Willows*; *Antigone*; *The John Wayne Principle* (also seen in London); *Beach Wedding*; *The Tempest*; *Treasure Island* and *Earth and Sky* starring Sam Janus, which also toured. Productions at the Warehouse Theatre: *Miss Roach's War*, *Capital Nights* and *Sherlock Holmes*. Tours include *The Great Gatsby*; *When Did You Last See Your Trousers?*; *Home Truths* and *Bazaar and Rummage*. For the Birmingham and London Stage Companies David has lit Mamet's *Speed-the-Plow* and *Oleanna*; *Lighting the Day*; *Bridges and Harmonies* and *Mademoiselle Colombe* which starred Honor Blackman. Other productions in London include *Horace* (Lyric Hammersmith); *The Yeats Season* (Hampstead); *Zanna* (Greenwich); Caracalla Dance Theatre's *An Oriental Night's Dream* (Peacock and worldwide) and currently *The Female Odd Couple* at the Apollo. Musicals include *Sweet Charity*, *Little Me* and *Grand Hotel* (Guildhall); *The Wiz* and *Tales My Lover Told Me*. In concert David has lit Monserrat Caballe and Joan Sutherland, both at Drury Lane. For four years David lit the London Pride Festival main stage and for three years

The Equality Show at the Royal Albert Hall, both events featuring major recording artists such as Elton John and George Michael. Recently David lit the *HSBC Youth Gala* performed by the National Youth Theatre, Ballet, Orchestra and Opera Studio at the Royal Albert Hall. Theme park and seasonal shows include *The Mask* (Butlin's) and *Peter Pan* (Legoland), and numerous pantomimes across the country. Television includes *Paul Merton Live!* at the Palladium and Neil Tennant's *The 20th Century Blues Gala*.

Marie Costa, Stage Manager

Marie trained at Mountview Theatre School before working as stage manager for the National Theatre of Cyprus. Since returning to England Marie has worked as stage manager, company manager and production manager. She has worked as stage manager and sound designer on over twenty productions at the Warehouse Theatre, including the International Playwriting Festival and Edinburgh Previews. She has worked with Sydney Theatre Company, Black Theatre Co-op, the Octagan Theatre, Bolton, Paines Plough, Performance Theatre Company, Red Shift and Sphinx Theatre Company. Other theatre work includes productions at the Drill Hall Arts Centre, Greenwich Theatre, the Young Vic Theatre, Riverside Studios, the Oval House, Brighton Festival and seasons at York Theatre Royal and the Thorndike Theatre, Leatherhead.

Paul Benzing, Fight Director

Paul has arranged fights for the likes of the RNT, the RSC, the Edinburgh International Festival, Theatre Royal Windsor, Bristol Old Vic and the Nuffield Theatre, where he has been involved in *The Wind in the Willows*, *Twelfth Night*, *The John Wayne Principle* and last year's Christmas show, *Treasure Island*, in which he also played Squire Trelawney.

The Warehouse Theatre was founded in 1977 in one of Croydon's few remaining Victorian industrial buildings and soon built a national reputation for producing and presenting the best in new writing. In 1986 it launched the prestigious International Playwriting Festival. Having inaugurated a partnership with the leading Italian playwriting festival, the Premio Candoni Arta Terme, in 1995, selected plays from the International Playwriting Festival are now seen at the festival in Italy as well as at the Warehouse, offering the potential for further performance opportunities in Europe. Last year saw a new international partnership created, with Theatro Ena in Cyprus. Previous winners such as Kevin Hood, whose play *Beached* won the first ever Festival, have gone on to achieve incredible success nationally and internationally. Kevin's two subsequent plays for the Warehouse, *The Astronomer's Garden* and *Sugar Hill Blues*, both transferred, the first to the Royal Court and the second to Hampstead Theatre. His most recent work includes the BBC2 series *In A Land Of Plenty*. Andrew Shakeshaft's *Just Sitting* was selected in 2000, and was showcased in Italy and in London in 2001. A full production is being planned.

Today the Warehouse Theatre is acknowledged as one of the foremost theatre's for new playwriting in the country. Other hugely successful productions have included *Sweet Phoebe*, by Australian playwright Michael Gow, which saw the London stage debut of Cate Blanchett, *Iona Rain* (winner of the 1995 International Playwriting Festival) and *The Blue Garden*, both by acclaimed playwright Peter Moffat and last year's critically acclaimed *The Dove* by Bulgarian playwright Roumen Shomov. A continuing success is the company's stage version of *Dick Barton Special Agent* by Phil Willmott. First produced at the Warehouse in December 1998 it was an instant success, was brought back by popular demand in 1999 and has been on almost continuous national tour since. A new production will open at the Nottingham Playhouse in September and will tour in the Spring of 2002. *Dick Barton Episode 2 – The Curse Of The Pharaoh's Tomb* was also an instant hit and a tour is planned. *Episode 3 – The Tango Of Terror* has been commissioned and will open at the Warehouse in December 2001.

Warehouse Theatre

Artistic Director: Ted Craig
Administrative Director: Evita Bier
Marketing Manager: Sarah Mallett
Assistant Administrator: Carolyn Braby
Education Coordinator: Rose Marie Vernon
Box Office Manager: Sharon Cowan
Production Manager: Graham Constable
Stage Manager: Marie Costa

Board of Management:
Cllr Brenda Kirby *chair*, Cllr Eddy Arram, Celia Bannerman, John Clarke, Tim Godfrey, Dr Jean Gooding, Mike Hodges, Michael Rose, Mia Soteriou, Cllr Martin Tiedemann, Cllr Mary Walker

Patrons:
Lord Attenborough CBE, George Baker, Lord Bowness CBE DL John Gale OBE, Joan Plowright CBE, Robert Stiby JP

Funding Bodies:
London Borough of Croydon
London Arts
London Borough Grants

Acknowledgements:

Warehouse Theatre Company are grateful for ongoing sponsorship from HSBC, Kingston Smith and Croydon Advertiser Group.

THE WAREHOUSE THEATRE COMPANY'S
INTERNATIONAL PLAYWRITING FESTIVAL

A National and International Stage for New Writing

This year the International Playwriting Festival celebrates sixteen years of discovering, nurturing and promoting the work of new playwrights, consolidating the role of the Warehouse Theatre Company as a powerhouse of new writing.

The play that you are watching today offers an example of the real success that writers can enjoy when their work is discovered by the International Playwriting Festival.

Maggie Nevill submitted *The Shagaround* to IPF 1999 and, following its selection from over 500 entries, Patrick Sandford directed a showcase presentation at the festival weekend. As the play was such an instant favourite with judges and audiences alike, it was then translated into Italian and presented in Udine at the IPF's partner festival, the Premio Candoni-Arta Terme, directed by Ted Craig.

The current co-production between the Warehouse Theatre Company and the Nuffield Theatre played a sell-out season at Southampton and a national tour is planned to follow this season at Soho Theatre.

The 16th International Playwriting Festival will take place at the Warehouse Theatre on Friday 23, Saturday 24 and Sunday 25 November 2001. Entries for IPF2002 will be received from January 2002.

The Dove

Sweet Phoebe

Dick Barton
Special Agent

NUFFIELD

NUFFIELD THEATRE SOUTHAMPTON

'Proof that high calibre work is still possible in our regional theatre'

(Michael Billington, The Guardian)

In 1960, the Nuffield Foundation donated £130,000 to the University of Southampton to help with the building of a new theatre for the city. This was finished in 1964 and was opened on 2nd March by Dame Sybil Thorndyke. Situated on the University of Southampton campus, the Nuffield formally separated from the University in 1982 and restructured its management into an independent trust. Its current Artistic Director, Patrick Sandford, joined the Nuffield in 1988.

One of the few remaining repertory theatres in the central southern region, the Nuffield has a commitment to presenting new writing and British premieres, notably of American and Australian plays that have included Woody Allen's *The Floating Lightbulb*, David Williamson's *Dead White Males* and most recently Tony MacNamara's *The John Wayne Principle* which was also seen at the Pleasance Theatre, London. Other recent premieres include *Spike* starring Richard Briers and Didier van Cauwelaert's French play *Noces de Sable* that received its premiere as *Beach Wedding* with Adrian Lukis and Nichola McAuliffe. Nuffield productions regularly tour and transfer to London, including recently *Earth and Sky* starring Sam Janus and Joe McGann.

The Nuffield has an important place in the local community, with a thriving education department that produces and tours children's theatre into schools and arts venues in the region and throughout the country. The next project this summer will be Hampshire Youth Theatre, a two-week workshop where the region's most talented 16-21 year olds work alongside the Nuffield Theatre Company towards a production on the main stage.

The Nuffield Theatre are delighted to be co-producing *The Shagaround* with the Warehouse Theatre Company, presenting the work of one of the many talented local writers in Southampton.

soho
theatre

Soho Theatre and Writers' Centre
21 Dean Street, London W1D 3NE
Admin: 020 7287 5060 Fax: 020 7287 5061
Box Office: 020 7478 0100 minicom: 020 7478 0136
www.sohotheatre.com   email: mail@sohotheatre.com

Bars and Restaurant   *Gordon's.*
The main theatre bar is located in Café Lazeez Brasserie on the Ground
Floor. The Gordon's® Terrace serves Gordon's® Gin and Tonic and a range
of soft drinks and wine. Reservations for the Café Lazeez restaurant can
be made on 020 7434 9393.

Free Mailing List: Join our mailing list by contacting the Box Office on
020 7478 0100 or email us at mail@sohotheatre.com for regular online
information.

Hiring the theatre: Soho theatre has a range of rooms and spaces for
hire. Please contact the theatre managers on 020 7287 5060 or email
hires@sohotheatre.com for further details.

stone

Gordon's

Bloomberg

TBWA\GGT DIRECT

A&B
Arts & Business

All our major sponsors share a common commitment to developing new areas of activity with the arts. We specifically encourage a creative partnership between Soho Theatre Company, the sponsors and their employees.

This translates into special ticket offers, creative writing workshops, innovative PR campaigns and hospitality events.

The **New Voices** annual membership scheme is for people who care about new writing and the future of theatre. There are various levels to suit all – for further information, please visit our website at:
www.sohotheatre.com/newvoices

Our new **Studio Seats** campaign is to raise money and support for the vital and unique work that goes on behind the scenes at Soho Theatre. Alongside reading and assessing over 2000 scripts a year, we also work intensively with writers through workshops, showcases, writers' discussion nights and rehearsed readings. For only £300 you can take a seat in the Education and Development Studio to support this crucial work.

If you would like to help, or have any questions, please contact the development department on 020 7287 5060 or at:
development@sohotheatre.com

We are grateful to all of our sponsors and donors for their support and commitment.

LONDON ARTS

SUPPORTED BY
CITY OF
WESTMINSTER

PROGRAMME SUPPORTERS

Research & Development: Anon • Samuel Goldwyn Foundation • Harold Hyam Wingate Foundation • Calouste Gulbenkian Foundation
Education: Delfont Foundation • Follett Trust • Hyde Park Place Estate Charity • Roger Jospé • Sainsbury's Checkout Theatre
Access: Bridge House Estates Trust
Building: The Rose Foundation
New Voices
Gold Patrons: Anon • Julie & Robert Breckman • David Day • Raphael Dyanoglj • Mr and Mrs Jack Keenan • Patrick Marber • Krister Rindell • Christian Roberts • Stagecoach Theatre Arts School (Chigwell) • Suzanna Barnes • Katie Bradford
Silver Patrons: Rob Brooks • Esta Charkham • Jonathan & Jacqueline Gestetner
Bronze Patrons: Davina & Larry Belling • John Drummond • Samuel French Ltd • Madeleine Hamel • Audrey & Geoffrey Morris • Alexander S. Rosen & Armand Azoulay • Nathan Silver • Paul & Pat Zatz
Studio Seats: Anon • Peter Backhouse • Leslie Bolsom • David Day • Imtiaz Dossa • Raphael Dyanoglj • Roger Jospe • John and Jean McCaig

The Italian Job

Maggie Nevill's journal, Italy 2000

TED, Artistic Director, Warehouse Theatre

EVITA, Administrative Director, Warehouse Theatre

THE BIG NOISE, FRANCO, Artistic Director of Premio Candoni-Arta Terme

RITA, actress playing Dilly

NICOLETTA, actress playing Lisa

ROBERTA, actress playing Beth

ILARIA, actress playing G

ARIANNA, actress playing Sal

FABIANO, actor playing Matt

MARK and PATRICK, Directors of Nuffield Theatre

"We're taking you to Italy!" says Ted

ME: To Italy?

TED: We're going to do the play in Italian!

ME: In Italian? Um...don't we have to speak Italian for that?

TED: Nah. It'll be a wheeze. We'll have interpreters and stuff. There's a terrific restaurant by the theatre. Do you like pasta?

ME: No. Not particularly, I think, experiencing an unpleasant flashback of my last thrice-microwaved Vegetarian Pasta bake. But I'm game for anything, and he must know what he's doing, being a director and that. It's not exactly easy to get a play on anywhere, so that if someone wants to premiere mine in Northern Italy, in Italian, who am I to cast the first spanner?

I set myself the awesome task of trying to purchase some sort of playwright's summer wardrobe from the bad-taste carnival of Southampton high street, fail dismally and await take-off, hoping to God I don't sit on my sunglasses.

Monday

I am crouching on my bed waiting for The Pifco Mini Water boiler to explode. It doesn't. I am so relieved. Italians serve coffee by the spoonful. I've tried at least ten ways of ordering it today and got no further than a gobful of tar in the bottom of varying sizes of cup. Now, at last, fortified by a homely Nescafe, I can start to acclimatise myself to the strange circumstances I find myself in, i.e., that of being an instant playwright in an entourage of Espresso theatre types who obviously do writing festivals for breakfast. Sitting opposite Fabiano earlier on, watching him debate some piece of the translation in Italian, I was suddenly struck with misplacement delirium and nearly laughed aloud.

This is a relief, as, for the last week at least, I have been suffering an insane amount of nerves about coming here, resulting in me bringing practically every item of clothing I own, just in case (or only – just in holdall), which I have now unpacked and sorted into piles of what I will and will not wear (about half and half). I had no idea that it would be this hot.

The *Shagaround* girls, however, are unanimously cool, I decide straight away, as we stand around smoking outside the fire escape, nodding at one another intercontinentally, and look as if locking anyone up in a toilet for real wouldn't worry them or their mascara. As we trot into the theatre, I feel as if the play might be in the right kind of hands.

Our first task is to check out the translation, with which object we all sit around on the stage and read the script. *The Shagaround* has been translated as *Lurido Schifoso Bastardo* which, apparently, means 'You dirty bastard' – a stylistic transgression, I think, but we leave it for now and tackle the text.

How do I know how the thing has been translated? I don't, but sniggers from the cast or mystified silences indicate a few obvious dead ducks. By the end of the afternoon we have axed the Musketeer jokes and 'Auld Lang Syne', replaced France with Slovenia and sifted out a multitude of hilarious English double-entendres which mean absolute squat in Italian, with only the briefest of sighs on my part. I'm slightly worried that my vast and carefully crafted variety of insults and expletives seem to have been reduced to *porco* and various versions of the word *Stronzo* but, having been formerly warned that Italian is short on slang and knowing of the English language's unexplained supremacy and richness of vocabulary when it comes to genital swear words, I don't know whether it's worth protesting too much, though the cast happily help us to filter and replace the *porco* percentage I find repetitive to the ear.

We manage to get through it all before dinner – an occasion which lasts almost as long as the rehearsal. I am too exhausted to try and communicate in careful English, so snaffle and quaff quietly and find out that Ted is a serious wine-taster. Told him I normally mixed red wine with soda and he nearly passed out.

Tuesday

We are hauled off at dawn to a town called Gorizia, to read the play to the students who initially translated it. The very idea of my play having been part of anybody's curriculum is bizarre enough and when I see the layout of the classroom and hear the youthful Italian chatter, it brings back an unwarranted memory of a similar situation; when I did a morning's work for an English language school and resigned instantly, owing to my suddenly realised lack of knowledge of the technicalities of my own language. Now here's a turnip for the books. They throw me completely by giving me an enthusiastic round of applause (not something my former students would have had any incentive to do). I can't decide what to do with my face, so let it twitch independently.

The cast start to read and I watch the class in wonderment. The front row girls seem increasingly outraged as the substitution of their *porcos* becomes apparent. It is the word they've more or less consistently used to replace Shagaround, so me and Ted try to explain that the Shagaround is more of a joke word and everybody battles to think of an Italian parallel. Roberta eventually comes up with the word *Il Trombatore* which (she says) is a pun on shabby sex, someone who plays the trombone and *La Traviata*. Me and Ted can only go on the fact that it sounds good and that we both think Roberta is cool. The class is divided, but nobody comes up with anything else, and so our new title is born.

I corner what appear to be the only three male students outside and ask them what they think of the play. One says that it is 'very modern' and that Italian women wouldn't use language like that. I wonder privately whether he can be so sure. Ted speaks to the females who, he says, aren't fazed by it at all.

We take *Il Trombatore* into the theatre in the afternoon and things get suddenly physical. Tables are upended. Mops are brought forth. I don't have to follow the script word for word any more and again get that feeling of weird surrealism, which is enhanced when I go outside at dusk to find that a terracotta glaze has painted itself over the sky, walls and shutters-peeling paint and old colours

– and that there is a soft foreign blush across everything. Inside again and Rita is falling backwards into the toilet, Nicoletta is looking hot and pissed off and everybody's clothes are getting dirty.

We have a discussion over dinner about the – alleged – poor quality of English cuisine, Evita suggesting that it may have to do with our – alleged – national lack of sensuality. Being the only English person at the table (Ted having sneakily turned out to be Australian), and being in the middle of my first indigenous pizza, I don't defend the issue with any great gusto, but take the idea back to my hot hotel room to ponder. Another sleepless night.

Wednesday

Bit of a tense day. Lots of stopping and starting and actors standing around looking bored. I decide to ignore the no-smoking signs in the auditorium as nerves (mine) and tensions (also mine) mount. Arianna has done her back in and is huffing and groaning all morning. She might well be pissed off that this *reading* has now got her climbing up and down a five foot door all day. She does the lipstick-on-the-wrists scene beautifully, however, bringing tears to my eyes, as does Ilaria when she gets dragged under the door. I have a little playwright's moment with myself.

We haven't finished moving Act Two by the end of the day, we're teching tomorrow and I'm already full of fingernails by the time we go to dinner. Spending half the day in restaurants is driving me crazy, but there's something delicious about the way Italian women eat: without the shame and apology one hears in England whenever a woman orders anything more calorific than a lettuce leaf. Evita may have a point about the sensuality thing, I think, watching them all wildly orgasm over the tagliatelle, as I wait for an appropriate moment to smoke.

They certainly don't look any the worse for it, either. There's something about the way Italian women present themselves that you can't argue with. They wear their bodies with pride, which is something our androgynous culture back home hardly encourages. This seems to me to be a truer feminism than the policy of de-sex. Why are the English always trying to take the sex out of everything? Why can't we have actresses and manageresses any more? Why are we calling people chairs? What are we afraid of? I've never before asked myself why the English language is genderless, but all this translation stuff has set me wondering. Is it a reflection of suppression or liberation? I wonder, necking my third grappa and gazing idly at the vine-tapestried sunset.

As we weave our way back through the quiet streets of Udine, I conclude that it's definitely worth thinking about sometime.

Thursday

"God, this is tedious", I think. Haven't I already done this once before? (lying on my floor at home for half an hour trying to decide what word to use. I am lying on the floor of the sweaty auditorium now while they decide what part of the stage to stand on while they say it). My legs are killing me from sitting around all day and I look like a bastard. I have more baggage under my eyes than I have in my wardrobe. My make-up fell off over breakfast.

More translation hiccups (nay, farts) are emerging today. Ilaria finally confessed that she didn't understand why she growls at Fabiano, something she's been awkward about doing all week. Investigation revealed that he isn't calling her a bitch at all, or that 'bitch' doesn't have anything to do with dogs any more. Also, we discovered that he tells Arianna he's shat in her boot, instead of

pissed in it. I thought this was hilarious, but Ted, more
sensibly, pointed out that it did nothing for realism.
Lurido Schifoso Bastardo has to stay in the programme, as
The Big Noise; Franco isn't around to give *Il Trombatore*
the seal of approval. Evita says that this is the worst
thing you can say to someone in Italian, so I assume my
play has adopted a title that begins with C and that
people don't say quite so much outside of Portsmouth.
"Who wrote the bloody thing?" I muttered over lunch,
but the matter was overshadowed by a heated debate as
to the correct order of salt, vinegar and oil when
dressing a salad.

We have been kicked out of the auditorium and shunted
into a rehearsal room upstairs, which is even hotter.
I make suggested cuts for Ted with astonishing
compliance, just hoping that we can run through the play
at some point in less than four hours.

We went further out into Cividale tonight for dinner,
Rita completely blowing my Italian Woman image by
taking slimming pills before she ate.

Friday

More mind-shaggingly slow rehearsal. Discovered that
my 'body like a fruit salad' has become a custard.
Nobody seemed to think there was much difference, and
I had to explain that the metaphor was supposed to
denote a kind of fresh and moist voluptuousness. Ted,
who'd had tinned fruit-salad in the hotel for breakfast,
was as bemused as the Italians. This is the point where
I realise that these actors could be saying anything and
what do I know? If the script were literally translated
back into English would I have an entertaining read or a
coronary? If we had another week or so, I would dig
deeper, but there's no time to be precious now, tomorrow
being D-Day. Nervoso? Me? Nobody else seems to be so

I try to form some semblance of calm. I have started to swear to myself in Italian.

The festival has started now and our formerly deserted lunchtime restaurant is full of theatre people and actors whom our cast all seem to know and need to kiss. Me and Ted are smiled at politely, and I wish furiously that I could speak. I feel like I'm bursting to the point of explosion with the amount of words I haven't spoken this week. I briefly picture them bursting out in a volcanic stream and peppering everyone's pasta.

The play seems to be getting itself together in the afternoon, and I am relatively confident that tomorrow won't be too much of a disaster by the time we break for the first Italian play. I take the opportunity to scurry back to the hotel for a shower and a brief attempt at a nap, making it back to the theatre in time to catch two guys rolling round in what look like lobster nets, clutching each other and shouting incomprehensibly. I decide that they are in the process of dying, but am informed afterwards that they were actually bewailing some sort of incestuous relationship with their sister.

We go into town to the first festival dinner where I finally get to meet Franco, who greets me with a melancholy *ciao*. We stand and look at each other for a moment and mutually decide to skip the kisses. He does, however, crack some sort of acceptance joke about *Il Trombatore* so that everyone looks relieved.

Saturday

I get to sleep until ten o'clock, I'm so happy. I consider skipping lunch and going for another couple of hours, but decide that lacks festival spirit and turn up just before the end of this morning's reading. Things are running late and our final rehearsal is being jeopardised by an insistence that we go to lunch with everybody else instead of just around the corner, which we'd like to do, as we only have half an hour (just about enough time for an Italian to unfold his/her napkin). Officialdom wins, of course, and the cast settle into their destiny, being the whole three courses and coffee. I am going mad with anxiety and actually bellow at one point that surely some things are more important than food? at which they all grace me with looks of amused pity.

We finally get out of there and back to our rehearsal room and I needn't have worried because they run through the entire play beautifully. I am choked with gratitude and everyone seems happy. All we have to do now is wait for a couple of hours to present our little gift to the people of Udine.

I flit back for a quiet scotch while everyone watches a play about resurrected babies. I am back outside the theatre at six o'clock, trying to look cool, when Patrick and Mark stroll along the road, as casually as if they popped over to see readings in Italy every day. More or less simultaneously, *The Dove* * cast turn up in a minibus and I find myself having to find something to say for the first time in a week . I feel like I'm speaking really slowly and reiterating everything with sign language. "Let's get it over with", I say (and gesticulate), as the appointed time comes, and we go inside the auditorium where there seem to be nobody but us and a couple of the students from Gorizia. Quarter of an hour later the Italians file in out of the sun, the lights go down, and Evita introduces the play. This is it then.

It's an excruciating experience, watching your own play. Or rather, watching other people watch your play. It's

* *The Dove* by Roumen Shomov was the other selected play in the IPF 1999. The play was produced at the Warehouse Theatre in May 2000 and the cast presented an edited version at the Premio Candoni Arta Terme.

like watching someone unwrap the Christmas present you've just given them and hoping they'll like it as much as you want them to. There's probably not an audience in the world who could look pleased enough. It all goes so fast, in a blur. I am conscious of every line that I've laboured so long over and painfully delivered, as they disappear into the thin air and die their little deaths. It suddenly dawns on me how stupid I have been – why have I made myself so ridiculously vulnerable? What ever made me want to parade my thoughts and feelings in front of a bunch of complete strangers like I am doing now? What on earth for? Why am I writhing about in this chair waiting for them to laugh at my jokes? Why would they? And who are all these crazy people who have let me – nay, encouraged me – to do it? And yet when they do laugh, when they do react, it's a feeling like nothing else. It's hallowed and scary. It's the compliment that's so personal and longed for, you could never be prepared for it, and I feel the most shy I've ever felt in my life at the moment and thank God I'm down here in the dark and not up there with those mad people called actors, who must be a different species to me because I could never do what they're doing now – I can't believe that they're doing all this for me – they hardly know me – are they crazy or what?

By the time we reach the sticky end, I am sure that I've lost about half my body weight in sweat, and half my credibility also, but then the audience claps, and someone cheers, and nobody's lobbing anything rotten at the stage, so I assume I've got away with it. This time. – Will it be like this every time? – Is it worth it?

Hell, I think, wringing out my shirt and mopping my tortured brow in the senores, somebody's got to do it. Because the one thing I am absolutely sure of is that theatre has got to exist.

We go to the cafe round the corner for a couple of beers before Mark and Patrick skit back to Venice and everybody else trickles back to the theatre and I tell Ted I'll just hang on for a minute and write a few things down. He nods and smiles as if this is the most natural thing in the world and, as I sit there with my glass of *refosco*, pen in one hand, fag in the other, it seems as if it is. I remember thinking a year or so ago that if I could only see a play of mine on the stage, my life would be complete. But that's not true, I find out. Because now I want more of it.

A piece of proper toast wouldn't go a miss either.

Maggie Nevill
June, 2000

First published in 2001 by Oberon Books Ltd.
(incorporating Absolute Classics)
521 Caledonian Road, London N7 9RH
Tel: 020 7607 3637 / Fax: 020 7607 3629
e-mail: oberon.books@btinternet.com

A catalogue record for this book is available from the British
Library.

ISBN: 1 84002 240 X

Cover photograph: Gemma Mount
Cover Design: Oberon Books
Series Design: Richard Doust

Printed in Great Britain by Antony Rowe Ltd, Reading.

Characters

BETH

SAL

LISA

DILLY

G

MATT

TWO WOMEN
(played by members of the cast)

For 'Sal'

Thanks to all at The Nuffield and Warehouse theatres, especially Patrick and Penny for their enormous help with the script, and to The Wild Women of Southampton for initiating it.

ACT ONE

A ladies' toilet in a pub. There are three cubicles lining the back of the stage. The front of the stage is an imaginary mirror. There is a door to the right of the cubicles that leads into the bar.

SAL is standing at the front of the stage, scrutinising herself in an imaginary mirror (which is, in effect, the audience). There is the sound of a toilet flushing and then BETH emerges from one of the cubicles and joins SAL.

SAL: Oh no, Where's it gone?

BETH: Where's what gone? What have you lost?

SAL: My face. It was there when I came out. Where is it now?

BETH: You look fine.

SAL: I look like shit. Honestly, I can't understand it. A couple of hours ago, I looked gorgeous. I could have shagged myself. I don't know how it happens. You never see it happening, do you?

BETH: What?

SAL: People's faces sliding off. Where do they end up? There should be a pile of them on the floor somewhere.

BETH: You look fine, for Christ's sake.

SAL: If you stood in front of a mirror all day, do you think you'd be able to see it happening? Could you catch it on film? You know, like one of those Andy Warhol films. *The Disintegration of a Face?*

BETH: That sounds more like a Dali painting. Andy Warhol would have just called it *Face.*

SAL: It looks a bit like a Dali painting, now you mention it. Kind of melted. I know it's the beer, I just don't know how it does it.

BETH: How can beer make your face slide off?

SAL: I don't know, that's what I'm saying. But look at Polly. She doesn't drink and she always looks amazing. She looks the same all night. Her eyeliner never runs. Her lipstick is practically black and it never comes off. She doesn't even get it on her glass.

BETH: She licks it first.

SAL: What?

BETH: The glass. It stops it coming off.

SAL: Does it? Why hasn't anybody ever told me that?

BETH: Nobody wants you licking their glasses.

SAL: Have you got any powder?

BETH: Yeah, but it's too pale for you. It'll make you look ill. (*Looks at her carefully.*) Iller. Have you slept lately?

SAL: I'd rather look ill than look like a snooker ball.

BETH: You'll look like a ping pong ball if you use this, seriously…

SAL: Give it to me.

BETH: Don't say I didn't warn you.

LISA comes through door from bar and runs into a toilet.

LISA: Hi there! Oh god, I'm bursting for a piss. I'll speak to you in a minute. (*She shuts the door.*)

SAL powders her face and surveys the result.

SAL: (*Groans.*) I look like a ghost.

BETH: You look a bit scary.

SAL: Don't say 'I told you so.'

BETH: I didn't.

SAL: I look like I've just puked. Have you got any lipstick?

BETH: You came prepared tonight then.

SAL: I wasn't going to come at all. I was in such a state. I couldn't find my bag. I couldn't find anything…

BETH: (*Sympathetically.*) Yeah, alright. I know.

SAL: I've got my tobacco stuffed down my boots, I've got a bloody tenner in my bra…

BETH: No way.

SAL: Yeah. It's itching like hell.

BETH: Just remember to take it out *before* you go and buy a drink – we don't want you spilling anything…

Sound of LISA scuffling around with the paper dispenser, an expletive.

SAL: Thanks for making me come out though…you know…

BETH: You can't stay in on New Year's Eve.

SAL: I know I've been acting really weird…

BETH: Well, we've all been there. So don't worry about it.

LISA's hand appears at the bottom of her cubicle door.

LISA: Is there any paper in the other toilet?

BETH fetches some without answering over following dialogue, throws it in over top of door.

SAL: I haven't even asked you about your week, have I? Was it horrible?

BETH: Casualty's always horrible, but it peaks at Christmas. Did I tell you about that guy and the nutcrackers?

SAL: (*Shuddering.*) Ergh, yeah. Was he all right?

BETH: (*Laughing.*) What do you think?

LISA: What guy with the nutcrackers?

33

SAL: (*Almost tearful suddenly.*) Look, thanks, anyway…

BETH: That's what big sisters are for, isn't it? (*Hugs her.*) Thank me by having a good time, okay?

SAL: (*Pulling herself together.*) I'll try. Where's G gone?

BETH: She went out in the garden.

SAL: Why? It's bloody freezing.

BETH: She saw Matt slipping out there for a piss or something. So she followed him.

SAL: What? That piece of shit? I thought they were finished? What's she doing?

BETH: Telling him what a piece of shit he is, I hope.

SAL: As long as she's not going back with him. Who was Dilly talking to?

BETH: Oh, one of their 'uni' friends. Rupert, would you believe? When I went to college, everyone was called Jackie or Mike. That's what happens when you do away with grants, I guess.

SAL: …This is red.

BETH: I know it's red.

SAL: I'm going to look like a geisha.

LISA emerges from toilet, still doing up the belt of her jeans.

LISA: God, that was close. Happy New Year!

BETH and SAL are unenthusiastic.

SAL: Have you got any lipstick?

LISA comes up to the mirror. Pulls a face at herself and looks away.

LISA: I thought I was going to piss myself. This ridiculous bloke has had me pinned against the bar for the last half an hour. I didn't think he was ever going to shut up.

BETH: Why didn't you tell him to shut up?

LISA: I was being polite. And I want him to fix my computer.

BETH: What's wrong with it?

LISA: Well I don't know, do I? Although he insisted on trying to tell me. In great detail. Honestly, you don't get anything for free, do you? I stopped having the faintest idea what he was talking about in the first five seconds. I could feel my eyes going all glassy.

BETH: Your eyes are all glassy. Are you pissed already?

LISA: I was. I just feel depressed now. He asked me to go round some time to play on his Playstation.

BETH: That is depressing. Did he say you could play with his joystick too?

LISA: No. I don't think that's what he meant. He was going on about getting to the third level.

BETH: I don't think I've ever been there. Perhaps you should go.

SAL: Are your lips the same as they used to be?

LISA: What do you mean?

SAL: I mean that lipstick is getting increasingly hard to put on. My lips don't seem to have an edge any more. Where did that go?

BETH: It must be on the floor with your face.

LISA: Do you think if I stay in here long enough, he'll go away?

BETH: If he thinks you're being sick, he might. Depends how much he wants to play with you.

SAL: I wonder if I can grow a beard to match this moustache…

BETH: Sal, relax, will you? You look okay.

SAL: No, seriously. Look at it from this angle… David Niven or what?

BETH: More of a Groucho Marx, I'll fetch you a cigar.

LISA: I can't see anything.

BETH: You won't, there's nothing there. It's a paranoiac hallucination.

LISA: Why? Have you taken something?

BETH: She's a bit low, aren't you, kid?

LISA: Why? What's happened?

SAL: Steve dumped me.

LISA: What? When?

SAL: Monday. The bastard. Got his Christmas present first, didn't he?

LISA: Why did he dump you?

SAL: He said he couldn't handle it.

LISA: Oh, they all say that nowadays though, don't they? They can't handle it. They need space. They need to be by themselves for a while. It's the cry of The New Age Man.

SAL: He handled every bloody inch of it first, though.

BETH: Piece of shit.

LISA: They're all so weird, aren't they? Don't you ever wish you could go out with someone like your Dad?

BETH: I think they've named a complex after that, Lisa…

LISA: I mean, someone with big shoulders who holds chairs out for you and can handle everything.

BETH: Except loading a washing machine, cooking, ironing, shopping, children…

SAL: Yeah. The only thing our Dad handles is the remote control. I think I'd rather go out with Mum.

SAL and BETH laugh.

LISA: (*To SAL.*) Is he here tonight?

SAL: What? Dad?

LISA: *Steve...*

SAL: Not yet, but he probably will be. Celebrating his freedom, no doubt. I don't really want to see him, but I didn't want to stay in either. Everything on the tele is so depressing all of a sudden, and everything reminds me of him. Somebody snogged on *Coronation Street* last night and I was so jealous – I couldn't bear the thought that somebody else was going to get a shag...

LISA: Do they shag on *Coronation Street* nowadays?

SAL: Like bunnies. They shag on everything. About the only thing on tele you can watch if you've just been dumped is the news, and they'll be shagging on that soon. (*Scrutinising face again.*) Oh, I give up. It's a landslide. Why should I look good? I haven't eaten or slept for five days. And who cares anyway? I hate New Year's Eve.

LISA: I know what you mean. If you're not with somebody you feel obliged to cop off, don't you? It all hinges around the midnight snog. You've got to be very careful who you're standing next to...

BETH: It sounds like you're already sorted out with Gameboy, Lisa...

LISA: God. He'll probably be drinking his cocoa by then.

SAL: He could have waited another week, couldn't he?

BETH: I think we're going to have to get some more beer down you.

SAL: I've had plenty of beer, it's all swashing round inside, I feel like a dishwasher.

LISA: Try Guinness. It's practically food.

The door to the toilet opens and G and DILLY come in quickly.

G: There you are! We've been looking for you everywhere. Go on, Dill.

DILLY: This is crazy.

DILLY, egged on by G, takes off a pair of long boots and then her tights. G does the same. The other women watch them, bemused. DILLY hands the tights to G, who gives them to BETH.

BETH: What's going on?

DILLY: She's gone crazy.

G: Hold these and don't go anywhere. Sal, come with us.

SAL: Why?

G: You'll find out

BETH: What am I supposed to do with these?

G: Hold onto them and be ready.

G and DILLY exit.

SAL follows with a shrug.

BETH contemplates the tights with distaste.

BETH: Christ. Your own tights are bad enough, but... somebody else's? What do you think she's up to? Do you think she's going to haul Matt in here and strangle him?

LISA: Why? What's Matt done now?

BETH: Jesus. Where have you been, Lisa? What little world do you live in? – *Matt's* been seeing somebody else. So G says. Though how he can see anything but his own kidneys with a head shoved that far up his arse, I don't know.

LISA: Who's he been seeing?

BETH: Nobody knows. But if you see a girl walking around with only one earring in, tell her to go home.

The door swings violently open and G crashes in with DILLY and SAL. They are hauling a struggling MATT between them. He is quite strong and it takes them a while to drag him into the room proper.

G: Well, don't just stand there!

LISA: I thought you were joking. Shit. You weren't joking.

BETH: What do you want us to do?

G: Get him in the cubicle – quick! Give me the tights, Beth!

MATT: Oi! Watch the bleeding jacket, will you?

BETH joins in. LISA looks confused. MATT is successfully shoved into the middle cubicle, (his jacket coming off in the process and falling to the floor), and the door is pulled shut. DILLY and SAL cling onto the handle. MATT bangs on it immediately, shouting the following lines over the ensuing action...

G? What the fuck? What are you doing?? Open this door!

G holds out a hand and BETH passes her the tights, which she ties around the handle and then to the handle of the third cubicle. She stands back.

G: Alright. That should do it. Let go now.

DILLY and SAL let go cautiously. MATT knocks on the door – sarcastically, as if knocking on a front door.

MATT: Hello?

G: Yes? Can I help you?

MATT: Okay. Very funny, G. What exactly are you playing at?

G: Fifty quid. That's what I'm playing at.

MATT: That bleeding fifty quid…What about it?

G: You owe it to me.

MATT: Yeah? So? You'll get it back. I just told you that.

G: I will get it back, or you're in there for the night.

MATT: I haven't got it on me, have I?

G: Oh dear. That's unlucky.

MATT: I told you I'll give it to you tomorrow.

G: No, Matt. I've had it with this. Every time I split up with
someone, they owe me money, and I never get it back.
You've owed me fifty quid for a month now and I want it
tonight. It's my New Year's Resolution, see?

MATT: G, I haven't got fifty quid. You can keep me in here
for as long as you like, I still won't have it.

G: Then your mates will have to lend it to you.

MATT: They won't, will they?

G: Then you're staying where you are.

MATT: What's got into you, all of a sudden? You don't care
that much about money.

G: No, I don't. It's the principle of the thing. You borrowed
money off me to fix your stupid, pathetic car, and I
bought you drinks and you smoked my fags because you
were always so skint, and all the time you've been
shagging someone behind my back. It's just taking the
piss. I'm sick of people taking the piss out of me.

MATT: Look, I haven't been shagging someone behind
your back…I just shagged someone once behind your
back, okay? …What do you mean, my stupid, pathetic
car?

G: Once? You expect me to believe that?

MATT: Okay, twice. What difference does it make?

G: (*Mimicking.*) 'What difference does it make?' You even let me go down the clinic again, didn't you? To get more stupid pathetic condoms to leave in your stupid pathetic bedroom. I want them back too. I don't want you using them on *her*.

MATT: Aren't you getting tired of this?

G: Did you use them on *her*?

MATT: No, She was on the pill, okay? You can have all your precious condoms back. Intact. Alright?

G: What? So you've probably given me some fucking disease now as well? Oh, Cheers, Matt. Thanks a lot. A hundred quid.

MATT: What?

G: It's just gone up.

MATT: Have you gone mad.

G: Yeah, I've gone mad. I'm mad as hell. A hundred quid. You'd better start hoping your mates really like you.

MATT: You're joking, right? Okay, good joke. Now, let me out.

G: Do I sound like I'm joking? Am I laughing?

MATT goes quiet for a moment and then starts rattling the door frantically.

The girls rush back over and lean against it.

DILLY: Do you think they'll hold out?

BETH: We could do with another pair…

The girls all look around. LISA and BETH are wearing trousers. Everyone looks at SAL, who has a short skirt and ankle boots on.

…Sal?

SAL: Oh, come on, guys, it's freezing. And I haven't shaved my legs.

MATT renews his assault on the door.

The girls shout various things at SAL

Bloody hell. Alright.

She removes her boots and then her tights and hands the tights to G who ties them around the door handles.

SAL rubs her legs peevishly.

SAL: How long are you going to keep him in there? I need the toilet.

G: As long as it takes. I'd go now if I were you.

SAL: I don't want to go with him listening.

G: Whistle then.

SAL: I can't whistle.

LISA: Sing?

SAL: I can't sing.

DILLY: Everyone can sing, for Christ's sake. What's got into you?

BETH: This is life in wartime, kid. You'd better just get on with it.

SAL hesitates.

DILLY: It is just a piss you want isn't it?

SAL: (*Appalled.*) Of course it is! Thank you, Dill...

A flustered SAL goes into the first cubicle and locks the door. She starts to sing in a weak, nervous voice. The other girls snigger and then shush each other.

MATT appears at the top of the second cubicle, having climbed up on the toilet.

SAL screams.

G picks up one of SAL's discarded boots and chucks it at him. It hits him on the head.

MATT: Ow! You bitch!

He glares at G, who threatens him with the other boot.

DILLY runs out quickly and returns with a mop. She climbs up the door of the third cubicle and brandishes it at MATT.

DILLY: Get down, Tiger.

MATT: What's this got to do with you?

DILLY: Girl power.

MATT: Fucking hell.

DILLY prods him with the mop and he obviously falls off the toilet. LISA looks thoughtful.

LISA: Has anyone got a screwdriver?

G: A screwdriver? Why would anybody have a screwdriver?

SAL: I bet Beth has.

BETH: Well, actually, yeah. I have.

LISA: Give it here a minute.

G: Why have you got a screwdriver?

SAL: She's always prepared for a screw.

BETH: To fix my bike lights, thank you, Sal.

She goes to bag and produces a screwdriver kit.

What do you want it for?

LISA: I've got an idea.

LISA assembles the screwdriver.

MATT tries to climb up again and DILLY hits him harder with the mop. He swears and goes back down.

MATT: You've got bleach on my shirt, you stupid cow. What's the matter with you?

DILLY: (*Threatening him again.*) You're outnumbered, punk. Start being nice.

G: Just cough up, you little shit, then we can all go back outside.

MATT: I'm not giving you anything now. It's New Year's Eve, G. Why can't you just wait till tomorrow, like any normal person?

G: Why should I ? How many paydays have gone past, Matt? I shouldn't have had to ask. You thought that I'd never speak to you again and you could get away with it, didn't you? Fifty quid. Thank you very much. Well, it takes me two days to earn that, and I've wasted enough fucking time on you already, so pay up.

MATT: (*After a pause.*) I've got a twenty. Take it or leave it.

G: It's a start. Put it under the door.

A twenty pound note comes out from under the door. G picks it up and pockets it.

MATT: So, are you going to let me out now or what?

G: When you've got the other eighty. Sure.

MATT: Look, I've fucking told you, haven't I?…

G produces a pen from her pocket and rolls it under the door.

G: You'd better write a little note to your friends then.

MATT: They're not going to give me eighty quid. Forget it.

G: We'll find out, won't we? Just write it, okay? Do you want us to tell you how to spell anything?

LISA: (*Knocking on the first cubicle door.*) Have you finished in there yet, Sal?

SAL: I can't go.

LISA: Well open the door. I need to come in.

SAL: I really want to go. I'm just too nervous.

LISA: Try in a minute then, when you're not so nervous.

After a brief pause, SAL comes out looking sheepish.

LISA goes into the toilet.

Give us a hand here, Beth.

BETH follows her into the toilet. They disappear behind the door. A piece of toilet paper comes out from under the door of MATT's cubicle. G picks it up and reads it.

G: '…come and break the door down, boys…the bitches have locked me in the toilet…D'.

SAL: Why D?

G: Him and his mates call themselves The Musketeers. Matt's D'Artagnan.

SAL: Are you kidding?

G: No. Sad, isn't it?

DILLY: Why is Matt D'Artagnan? Isn't he supposed to be the good looking one?

G: Matt is *D'Artagnan* because he plays *darts.*

Pause while everyone digests this information. Then they all laugh uproariously.

BETH: (*From inside toilet.*) Most men could be Aramis then…

G: Why's that?

BETH: Because they're expensive, they smell and they come in a box.

They laugh again. G screws up MATT's note and throws it into his cubicle.

G: Try again, Matt.

SAL: Where are my boots?

G hands over the remaining boot guiltily. The first toilet door drops off it's hinges with a clatter. They all look round.

LISA: Somebody give us a hand, will you? This is bloody heavy.

SAL and G go over to help. They all try to lift the door with much noise and giggling, so that when MATT suddenly grabs the end of DILLY's mop and pulls it hard, bringing her and the mop down inside his cubicle, nobody notices. The other girls lift the first cubicle door up and slide it over the top of the second cubicle. LISA and BETH climb from first toilet and onto the top of the door and sit on it. They shake hands, laughing. There is a pause, as they realise that someone's missing.

LISA: Where's Dilly?

G: What?

There is a muffled squeak from inside MATT's cubicle.

BETH: Oops…

SAL: He's got Dilly in there too!

G: (*To door.*) Dill?

Silence. The girls look worried. They don't know what to do.

Dill? Are you alright?

There is another noise, as if MATT has his hand over DILLY's mouth.

What are you doing to her? If you so much as touch her, Matt McGarry…you let her go!

MATT: Open the door and I'll let her go.

BETH: Maybe you'd better…

G is undecided. She looks around at everyone else. They shrug and then nod unhappily. G goes to the door handle as if to untie the tights. MATT screams.

MATT: You cow! You fucking bit me!

There is a sound of scuffling from inside the cubicle and then DILLY's arms emerge under the door.

DILLY: Grab my arms!

G: You'll never get under there!

DILLY: I will. I've done it before. I got locked in here once. Get off of my feet, fuckwit!

There is the sound of more scuffling and kicking.

SAL and G grab DILLY's arms and pull.

Ow!

MATT: Give up, girlies. Open the door now.

DILLY: Don't you dare. Pull, dammit!

LISA and BETH scramble down from the door and grab onto the back of G and SAL and also pull. DILLY's head comes out under the door. She is obviously in some pain. BETH lets go and goes over to her bag. She gets out a can of bodyspray. She lies down on the floor by DILLY's head and sprays it over her neck and into the cubicle.

MATT: What the fuck? What was that?

BETH: (*Reading the can.*) Vanilla Musk.

DILLY slithers out from under the cubicle door. She lies on the floor. They all look relieved and exhausted. BETH runs back up to sit on door top, just as MATT realises there's no-one on it and gives it a bang. It wobbles a bit. She signals to SAL to join her. LISA and G clap and cheer.

MATT: I smell like a cake, you bitches.

The girls get to their feet gradually, laughing.

G: Are you going to write the note now, Matt?

DILLY: Yeah, Come on, D'Artagnan…

SAL and BETH bang on the door with their fists and feet.

MATT: Alright, alright. Stop the fucking racket, will you?

Everyone cheers.

G: (*Pulling MATT's twenty out of her pocket.*) I think somebody should go and get some drinks with this (*She hands the note to LISA.*)

LISA: What does everybody want?

G: Does anybody not like wine?

General shaking of heads.

Just get a couple of bottles and some glasses then.

MATT: You'd better not be spending my money on wine…

G: It's my money, fuck off.

MATT: (*Suddenly pleading.*) Get us a pint of lager, will you?

Everyone laughs.

G: Hang on, Lisa. Have you written the note yet, Matt?

MATT: (*Softly.*) Bitch.

Pause, and then another piece of toilet paper comes out from under the door. G picks it up and reads.

G: 'Boys…need thirty quid. Lend us it. Will pay you back. Explain later, Matt…'

BETH: What happened to D'Artagnan?

G: What's a hundred minus twenty, Matt?

MATT: Come on, G…

G: What's a hundred minus twenty, Dilly?

DILLY: Eighty, G.

G: That's what I thought. Jesus, he's thick, isn't he?

MATT: I'm not giving you a hundred quid. Fuck off.

G: Have you got a pen in your magic bag, Beth?

BETH: Sure. Help yourself.

G gets a pen from BETH's bag. Changes the thirty to eighty.

G: I think this is ready to go then.

MATT: If you think you're getting a hundred quid out of me, you're a mad bitch…

G: Yeah, whatever. Do you mind delivering the ransom note, Lisa? I'd better stay in here with The Shagaround…

LISA: No problem. (*LISA takes the note from G, and exits.*)

G produces some cigarettes and offers them around. They light up.

MATT: Pass in my cigarettes, will you? They're in my jacket.

G: Oh good. I've only got a couple left. (*G pockets his cigarettes.*)

MATT: G… (*She blows smoke under his door evilly.*)

DILLY: What if The Musketeers won't cough up?

G: I haven't thought that far ahead.

SAL: I really need to go to the toilet now…

G: Matt? Will you stick your fingers in your ears so that Sal can go to the toilet, please?

MATT: Fuck off.

BETH: We'll sing then, won't we girls?

G: Yeah. Go on.

SAL climbs down and goes in first cubicle.

DILLY gets up in her place. SAL goes to shut door and realises there isn't one. Looks terribly flustered but obviously has to go. Wriggles pants down self-consciously.

SAL: What if somebody comes in?

BETH: They'll have to piss in the sink, won't they?

G: What'll we sing?

DILLY: 'Pissing in a river'?

BETH: Who's that by?

DILLY: Patti Smith.

BETH: Don't know it.

G: 'Yellow River'?

BETH: No wait…

SAL: Hurry up, for Christ's sake…

BETH: (*Singing.*) All we are saying…

DILLY (*Cottoning on.*) & BETH: …Is give piss a chance…!

They fall about laughing. SAL finally manages to go. It is audible.

MATT: (*From inside, singing.*) Drip drip drop little April showers…

BETH: (*Banging door.*) Shut it, you. (*Excitedly.*) …I know, I know! (*Singing.*) …Wee will wee will rock you!

All girls sing this, with floorslaps, handclaps.

BETH and DILLY mercilessly bang the door.

MATT: Leave it out!

They stop. Laugh again.

G: (*Singing.*) Urine my heart, urine my soul…

Round of applause from others.

SAL: It's okay, I've finished now!

BETH: Squeeze a bit more out Sal. We're just getting going!

LISA comes in with a tray of glasses and two bottles of wine. SAL comes out of cubicle.

G: Well? What did they say?

LISA: They laughed

MATT: They what?

LISA: They laughed and said he probably deserved it. (*She hands out glasses to everyone, then follows round with the wine.*) Sparky said that Matt'd do anything to dodge his round…

MATT: You're lying

LISA: …and Dave said he'd give us a fiver if we kept him in here all night…

MATT: Bastard.

BETH: So what do we do now?

LISA: Stay in here and drink the wine. There's not much going on out there yet.

SAL: (*Hesitantly.*) Is Steve here?

LISA: (*Also hesitantly.*) Yeah.

SAL: Who's he with?

LISA: His flatmate, I think.

SAL: Which one?

LISA: I don't know her name…

SAL: Is she short and blonde with a body like a fruit salad?

LISA: Yeah.

SAL: *Karen.* I hate her.

BETH: They're just mates, aren't they?

SAL: I still hate her. She never liked me either. I bet you fucking anything they get together.

BETH: You're paranoid. I thought you said he wanted space?

G: Oh yeah. When a bloke says he wants space, it means he wants someone else. He wants a free space in his fucking bed.

BETH: Woah.

G: Shit. Sorry, Sal. At least he split up with you first.

MATT: (*Quietly.*) That's what you think.

SAL: (*To door.*) What do you mean?

G: Shut up, Shagaround.

DILLY: (*Hastily.*) Shall I propose a toast?

BETH: Go on.

DILLY: Here's to the success of our venture. We don't give up yet, right, G?

MATT: You can't stay in here all night…

G: Oh, I don't know. I quite like it in here. I don't mind. Cheers everyone!

EVERYONE: Cheers!

SAL: What did you mean, that's what I think?

MATT: Are you talking to me?

BETH: Ignore him, Sal. He's winding you up.

MATT: Yeah, right.

SAL: I want to know what he means

G: Sal, Matthew is a liar. That's why he's in the toilet.

LISA: Do you think that all men are liars?

SAL: Steve wasn't a liar…

DILLY: No?

LISA: I mean, not exactly liars, but…able to say things that aren't true.

BETH: Is there a difference?

LISA: Well yeah. I mean… I'm not even sure they know they're doing it. Because they don't think there's anything wrong with it, see? Like…when they tell you things just because they think you want to hear them…

G: (*Directed at door.*) Oh yeah, like, 'I love you', 'We'll be together forever' …that sort of thing?

SAL: Steve said that too.

LISA: Yeah. It's like they think they have to.

MATT: (*Snorting.*) We do have to! Women are so paranoid! If you don't tell them you love them every night they think you've gone off them! If you don't tell them they look gorgeous every five minutes, they won't even leave the house! They always think you fancy someone else…

DILLY: (*Banging on the door.*) Who asked you?

G: They always do fancy someone else.

MATT: And women don't I suppose?

SAL: I didn't fancy anybody else.

MATT: I bet you did.

SAL: I bet I didn't.

MATT: I bet you've thought about somebody else since you split up with Steve.

Pause. SAL looks uncertain.

You have, haven't you? It's human nature. There's always somebody else. It's back-up, isn't it?

DILLY: What?

BETH: I don't know. He could be right.

G: Beth!

SAL: Yeah… You're attracted to other people, okay. But you don't actually fancy them. It's just a sort of physical thing but don't want to do anything about it. Not if you're with somebody you really like.

MATT: That's what you think. Other people's girlfriends flirt with me all the time.

G: No. You just think they do.

MATT: I know they do.

DILLY: You're just an arrogant pig.

LISA: There's a guy I know at work, right, who told me that he knew how much I fancied him because I'd brushed my left breast against his back at a party once…

BETH: Right. Because that's what we all do if we fancy a bloke, eh girls?

LISA: Exactly. I mean, would anybody really do that?

MATT: Yes.

DILLY: In your dreams…

LISA: What really amazed me, thinking about it afterwards, was that he remembered which breast it was. I mean, how would he know, anyway? If I rubbed it against his back?

G: What did you say to him?

LISA: I told him I was probably shoved.

BETH: Is that all?

LISA: I was too gobsmacked to say anything else at the time. But then I felt really insulted. That he thought I was actually sad enough to have done that…

DILLY: Well they don't see it as sad, do they? He probably thought you were being emancipated…

BETH: …girl makes her move…

DILLY: You should have told him to get a grip

BETH: Er…perhaps not, Dill.

They laugh.

You're too polite, Lisa.

LISA: I know. I find it terribly hard to turn anybody down.

G: So does Matt. In fact, he finds it so hard, that he doesn't.

MATT: Oh, lay off.

G: Is she one of your mates girlfriend's, Matt?

BETH: What mates? He's little Matty-No-Mates, aren't you? What happened to all for one and one for all?

MATT: I expect they thought you were joking.

LISA: That'll be why they're all laughing then.

MATT: They don't realise how mad you all are.

G: Well then, you'd better tell them. Write another note.

DILLY: Shall we cut one of his ears off and send it out as well? Have you got a scalpel in your bag, Beth?

BETH: I've got a Swiss army knife.

DILLY: That'll do. Has it got one of those little saw blades?

MATT: Steady on…

G: Are you writing?

MATT: How do you spell psychopaths?

Another note is pushed under the door.

G: (*Reading.*) 'I think they're serious. They're all crazy. Rescue needed. D'

BETH: Oh, he's D'Artagnan again, look.

LISA: He's appealing to his troops

DILLY: He's got to be appealing to somebody, the poor duck.

G: What do you think? Will it do?

SAL: (*Unhappy, disinterested.*) It doesn't mention the money.

G: True. (*Writes on note.*) 'Lend us the cash and I'll see you alright tomorrow, okay?'

LISA: Can you do his writing?

G: A five year old could do his writing. Who wants to take it out?

SAL: I think I will.

BETH: Sal, don't.

SAL: I just want to see what's going on, that's all.

BETH: I'm coming with you then. Who wants to sit up here?

LISA: I will.

They swap places and LISA goes up on the door.

SAL: Where's my other boot?

G: Shit, sorry, Sal. It's in there. I forgot about that.

MATT: I've pissed in it.

SAL: You haven't!

MATT: I will do, if you don't let me out.

SAL: (*Worried.*) Would he, G?

G: Well, he pissed all over me, I wouldn't put it past him. (*To MATT.*) If you piss in Sal's boot, it's a hundred and fifty.

MATT: Yeah, right.

G: If you pass it out now, I'll let you off at ninety-five.

MATT: Seventy-five.

G: Ninety.

MATT: Eighty.

G: Eighty five. That's my final offer. Take it now or we're back on a hundred.

MATT: Yeah, whatever. It smells of tights anyway.

The boot is kicked out under the door.

G: Oh, you're *such* a gentleman.

> *SAL checks the inside of the boot for piss and then puts it on. Looks down at her legs anxiously.*

SAL: Do my legs look really bad?

BETH: Hideous.

SAL: I mean, can you tell I haven't shaved them?

BETH: They don't need shaving, they need mowing.

SAL: Beth, I'm serious.

BETH: Do you want to go out there or not?

> *SAL looks around, sees DILLY's long boots.*

SAL: Dill? …Could I…?

DILLY: Jesus Christ. (*DILLY takes off her boots and swaps them with SAL during following dialogue.*)

G: Pour his pint over his head, Sal.

BETH: Don't give him the satisfaction. You're going to be cool, aren't you, Kid?

DILLY: It's a shame we haven't got any more tights – there's room for one more…

LISA: Couldn't we do something with the roller towel?

BETH: Will you stop it? Are you ready, Sal?

> *SAL looks at herself in the mirror and breathes deeply.*

BETH: You look gorgeous, okay?

> *SAL and BETH exit.*

LISA: Poor old Sal. She really liked Steve, didn't she? She was only with him for a couple of months. It doesn't seem fair. And at Christmas too.

DILLY: Well that's the best time to stuff a turkey, isn't it? Better to find out what a wanker he is after a couple of months than wait years for it.

LISA: I can't imagine going out with anyone for years. The most I've ever managed is one and a half.

G: Dilly was married for ten, weren't you, Dill?

LISA: Were you? I didn't know that.

DILLY: Why should you? It's all in the past. Thank God.

LISA: Wow. You always seem so…

DILLY: So what?

LISA: I don't know. So independent. I can't imagine you being married.

DILLY: I'm independent *now*. I learnt my lesson. I served ten years of a life-sentence and that was enough for me. I'm not going back.

LISA: Was it that bad?

DILLY: Yes. You don't realise how much you're going to change between twenty and thirty. I was much too young. So was Jimmy. Trouble was, he didn't change at all.

LISA: I'm glad I'm not with the person I was with when I was twenty.

DILLY: Exactly

LISA: He was crap in bed, for a start. I didn't have an orgasm till I was twenty-five.

DILLY: No way…

LISA: Really. I thought I had. Or I thought I might have. But you can't actually tell until you do, can you? And then I thought, Wow, this is it, I'm going to stay with you forever… but he turned out to be a one-night-stand. I was gutted.

DILLY: I hope you've had one since.

LISA: I don't think I've ever had one that was quite so good. I can remember it vividly.

G: I think I've had about three that I remember vividly. The rest were all kind of ordinary.

MATT: You bloody liar!

G: I was faking it.

MATT: You were not!

G: Not all the time. Sometimes. I don't mean I've only had three orgasms, I just mean that there's only been three that stand out. You know – that have sent me through the ceiling. And, before you ask, no, none of them were with you.

MATT: Well you're bound to say that now, aren't you? Who were they with then?

G: I'm not going to tell you that.

MATT: Because you can't.

G: You're not actually all that good in bed, Matt.

MATT: You never complained.

G: Well, no, I wouldn't, would I? I'm too shy.

MATT snorts.

(*To girls.*) Do you know what I mean though? Some men ask you what you want them to do, but how can you answer that? It's too embarrassing.

DILLY: They all like to think they're mechanics, don't they? Just tell them to look for a red button and turn it on.

LISA: What I hate are the ones who say, 'have you come yet?' I mean, they should know, shouldn't they? If they don't know you have then the chances are you haven't. And then by saying it, they make a big deal out of it, and then you can't anyway.

Girls murmur assent.

MATT: And just how are we supposed to know? I mean, some girls don't make any noise at all.

G: My nose runs when I do.

LISA: I usually laugh. They hate that.

MATT: I should think they do.

LISA: What's wrong with laughing?

MATT: I expect they think you're laughing at them.

LISA: Why should they? Sex should be fun. It *should* be a laugh.

MATT: You don't know what it's like being a bloke…

DILLY: (*Sarcastically.*) Oh, tell us about it, you poor old thing…

MATT: You're under pressure all the time. Women expect you to know exactly what they like and what they don't like, some women bite your head off if you try anything different, some women get bored of you if you don't…

DILLY: …I told my husband I wanted to experiment with food, so he came back the next night with an Indonesian take away. That's when I decided to divorce him.

LISA: You should have smeared him with hot peanut sauce…

DILLY: I'm allergic to nuts.

MATT: Bollocks!

DILLY: No, just peanuts.

MATT: Why didn't you just get on with it? Why did it have to be him who took the top off the yoghurt pot? I mean, there's nothing to stop the woman taking the initiative is there?

G: Yes there is, because a man thinks you're a slut if you do.

MATT: Rubbish. I'd love it.

G: You wouldn't.

MATT: How would you know? You always let me do all the work. You never ever took the initiative. Oh, and by the way, G, since we're having the old truth session here, you're not all that good in bed either.

An awkward silence. Everyone looks a bit embarrassed. At this point BETH and SAL return. SAL looks agitated.

SAL: Come on, you saw how they were talking. He's with her, isn't he?

BETH: I don't know, Sal.

SAL: He looked really embarrassed, the bastard. So he should be. Five days!

BETH: Maybe he's just embarrassed because he knows he's hurt you and he hasn't seen you till now. I don't know.

SAL: Did you see her face? She looked embarrassed too.

BETH: Well, Christ, I was embarrassed. It doesn't mean I'm shagging you, does it?

SAL: Do you think I'm being paranoid?

BETH: I don't know.

G: How did you get on?

BETH: I think they've got the message now. They're talking about it.

MATT: Talking about it? Look, go out there and tell Mickey he owes me a tenner anyway. And tell them I'm not exactly having a fucking laugh in here.

BETH: Will do.

MATT: No hang on, you go Lisa. Mickey fancies you.

LISA: Will that make a difference?

G: Probably, knowing Mickey. Do you mind going again?

LISA: No, it's alright.

G: If he pays out, get another bottle will you? We're almost dry here. In fact, get another one anyway, I've got some money.

MATT: Oh, you're loaded, aren't you?

LISA: Okay.

LISA exits.

BETH gets on the door.

SAL rolls a cigarette.

SAL: (*Banging on MATT's door.*) Tell me what you meant about Steve.

MATT: Give me a cigarette.

SAL: (*To G.*) Can I?

G shrugs.

SAL pushes the cigarette she's just made under the door.

MATT: This is a fucking roll up!

SAL: *And*? Do you want a light?

MATT: Alright.

SAL: Tell me first.

MATT: (*Sighing.*) Look, it's nothing. Steve nearly had a thing going with Karen before he met you, alright? He was thinking about it when you jumped in.

SAL: Jumped in?

MATT: Well, you came on to him, didn't you?

SAL: He could've said no.

MATT: Well he didn't, did he? I think Karen was pretty pissed off about it, at the time. But I don't think he was seeing her when he was seeing you. I was only winding you up. Can I have a light now?

SAL: So, in fact, he fancied Karen all the time that he was with me?

MATT: I don't know, do I? I expect she was…like I say… back up.

SAL: Back up! For Christ's sake!

MATT: I don't know what you're so mad about. He's split up with you, hasn't he? It's none of your business what he does now.

SAL: I'm mad because I feel like I've been taken for a complete ride.

MATT: Why?

SAL: Because he told me they were just friends.

MATT: He wasn't going to tell you anything else, was he? No man is 'just friends' with a woman. That's bollocks. That's just something that women like to believe. Can I have a light now, please?

SAL: No. Fuck off, Shagaround. I hate fucking men. All of them. You're all bastards.

MATT: Jesus Christ.

SAL: He even told me he didn't like big tits and look at hers…Christ, even *I* want to put my face in them…

SAL rolls a cigarette for herself and the others sit around drinking, smoking etc. A woman walks into the toilet and picks her way across the floor, looking a little confused. She looks at the first cubicle, with no door and then the second and third, tied together. She turns to BETH.

WOMAN: Is there somebody in there?

BETH: Yeah.

WOMAN: What about that one?

BETH: Well, no, but you'll have to climb into it. We can't open the door.

MATT: Is there somebody there? A normal person?

WOMAN: Who's that?

G: My ex. He's a wanker.

MATT: They're holding me prisoner. They're all psycho man-haters.

G: He two timed me and he owes me fifty quid. We're not letting him out till he pays it back.

WOMAN: Fair enough. Are there any other toilets in here?

G: There's some in the public bar.

WOMAN: Okay. Good luck.

MATT: Oi, hold on! What do you mean, fair enough? Come back here!

The woman smiles and exits. Matt is now getting pissed off.

I don't fucking believe this…

DILLY: Give up, Matt. Everybody hates you.

BETH: Are you alright, Sal?

SAL: No. I'll never be alright again. I feel so stupid. I wish I could be angry like you, G.

G: You will be, give it a few more days.

SAL: I might go home, Beth.

BETH: What for?

SAL: I've got a bottle of whisky at home.

BETH: You want whisky, we'll get you whisky.

DILLY: I started drinking whisky when me and Jim split up. I've had a bottle in the house ever since. Which is okay. It's better company than him. It tastes better too.

G: Don't go home, Sal.

BETH: No, come on, Kid. I know it's hard, but you've got to face it sometime…Steve's a shit.

SAL: He's not a shit!

DILLY: What is he then?

LISA returns, she has a bottle of wine.

LISA: Mission accomplished.

G: Is that from Mickey?

LISA: Yep.

BETH: Did you rub your left breast against him or what?

LISA: ...and...

G: There's more?

LISA: There's a tenner from Sparky. But he says, if you
    don't pay him back by tomorrow night, Matt, he's going
    to shag your little sister.

BETH: Nice.

G: There's your bottle of Scotch then, Sal.

SAL: For a tenner?

G: Yeah. From Metaxa Billy. He's got a load of stuff from
    France in his car. Well, nobody's going to see us drinking
    it in here, are they?

DILLY: Good thinking. I'll go and ask him. Give us your
    bag, Beth – so they won't see me bringing it in.

G: Can you get us some fags whilst you're out there, Dill?

DILLY: Sure. Anybody else want anything?

MATT: You could get me a fucking beer.

DILLY: Yeah, right.

G: Cheer up, lover boy. Only another forty five quid to go.
    You could still make it out for midnight.

MATT: You're a bitch, G.

G: I'm a bitch, I'm mad, I'm crap in bed. I don't know what
    you ever saw in me, Matt.

DILLY exits.

LISA gets up on the door in her place.

MATT: You could at least give me a fucking light.

G: What do you think, Girls?

BETH: Give him a light, but not a drink. We don't want him pissing in the ladies. It'll go all over the seat.

G: Good point. Okay, Shagaround. You can smoke.

She pushes a lighter under the door, as she does, MATT grabs her hand and pulls her into the cubicle up to her elbow.

Ow! Let go!

MATT: No way.

G: Let me go, you bastard!

MATT: This has gone far enough, G. You've had your little joke. You've got forty quid. Now, it's New Year's Eve, I want a drink, and I'm not pussying around any more. Let me out or I'll break your fucking arm.

G: You're hurting me!

MATT: I can hurt you a lot more. Are you going to let me out?

G, quite suddenly, starts to cry. She sobs noisily.

SAL: Let her go, you pig.

G: Go on then, break my arm… I'm not going to give in. Just for once in my life, I want to win. I'm sick of being ripped off by men…I'm sick of it! Look at this…a couple of weeks ago, we were lovers…a couple of weeks ago we were in bed together…how fucking close can you get?… and I trusted you…I fucking loved you…and you were lying to me…you were lying to me with your body and now you're going to break my arm…it all happens too fast. I can't handle it.

MATT: I'm not going to break your arm, for Christ's sake.

MATT releases her arm. G sits back up but continues to cry.

Will you stop crying G?

Pause.

Look, I'm sorry, okay?

G: Yes, but *why* are you sorry?

MATT: I'm sorry it didn't work out between us. I'm sorry I cheated on you. It just happened. Haven't you ever cheated on anybody?

G: (*Still sobbing.*) No.

MATT: (*Desperately.*) Haven't any of you?

SAL: No.

Pause.

SAL and G look at LISA.

LISA: I have, actually, yes.

MATT: Beth?

She rolls her eyes upwards, saying nothing.

He bangs on the roof door, underneath her, she jumps.

BETH: Well... Yeah, alright. I have too.

SAL: Have you?

BETH: Only for one night, you know...

SAL: Who did you cheat on? Not Pete?

BETH: No. Do you remember James?

SAL: James? He was really nice!

BETH: Yeah, I know. It was bad I suppose... But...well, I was staying with some old friends for a weekend and then this guy turned up who I'd always really liked and... I wasn't *intending* to...but you know how it happens...

She looks at the others. SAL and G don't know how it happens.

…I mean, James would never find out, so it didn't really matter and… (*She fizzles out.*) …Back me up, Lisa…

LISA: I went out with someone at college while I was still seeing someone at home…I didn't tell either of them.

MATT: Ha! There you go! It's not just men is it? Admit it! Women do it too!

G: Women don't do it to me.

MATT: They would if you were gay.

G: Thanks a lot.

MATT: What I'm saying is that women are just as bad as men, and yet as soon as someone dumps on them it's fucking men this, fucking men that, we hate fucking men, they're all pigs…and you all get together and agree with one another about how men are such bastards and half of you have done exactly the same thing…it's hypocritical.

G: Men do the same thing, I've heard them. All women are bitches…all women are whores…it's just the same.

LISA: There's something wrong with it all, isn't there?

SAL: I don't hate men, I just hate the ones that hurt me. It's only men that hurt me because it's only men I sleep with, therefore it's only men I really get to hate. But not all of them.

MATT: Now we're getting somewhere. Do you hate me?

SAL: I don't like you enough to hate you.

MATT: So why are you all ganging up on me? This should be between me and G. How would you feel, Beth, if me and this James locked you up in a toilet?

LISA: If it was a men's toilet she'd probably feel queasy, to say the least…

BETH: I didn't owe James any money...

MATT: Oh, come on, this isn't about the money, is it?

G: You don't understand the money thing, do you? It just annoys me. It's like you took me for even more of a ride. I keep thinking about it. And I want to think about something else, Matt. I want to start this New Year right, you know? Cut off the loose ends. Start again.

MATT: Okay, G, but just take another ten. I only owe you fifty quid, so take fifty quid and let's call it quits. My arse is starting to get a serious ring around it.

LISA: You're sitting on the toilet?

MATT: Well, funnily enough, yeah...there isn't a sofa in here.

BETH: I hope you've got your trousers up.

MATT: What do you say, G? Another ten quid and we'll call it quits, okay?

G: Oh, alright. Where are you going to get ten quid from?

There is a pause and then a ten pound note comes out under MATT's door.

You had it all along? You said you only had twenty!

MATT: Well, I had to get a round in when I got out, didn't I?

At this point another woman, well dressed and sophisticated looking, starts walking into the toilet.

G: I don't believe it! I just don't believe you, McGarry! You care more about drinking and about your mates than you do about me! You're such a shit heap!

MATT: G...G... You've got the tenner now. Forget about it, okay?

BETH: Ooh, I don't know about this...there should be some sort of penance for that kind of trick, don't you think, girls?

MATT: Shut the fuck up, Beth. This has got nothing to do with you.

WOMAN: On the contrary, darling -This has got something to do with all of us…

She walks onto centre stage, takes her shoes off and then her tights. The girls watch her with amazement.

(*To girls.*) I hope you don't mind?

They shrug. The woman goes over to cubicle doors and ties her tights around the door handles on top of the others.

It's a gesture. I was two-timed for a year, can you believe that? And he cost me a hell of a lot more than fifty pounds. If I knew where he was I'd love to do what you're doing now. They're all talking about it in the other loos. We're all behind you. Bloody men. They deserve everything they get. (*She bangs on the door.*) Are you listening to this, sweetie? I hope you're learning your lesson in there! (*She exits as abruptly as she came.*)

The girls are silent for a moment.

LISA: Wow.

G stares at the tenner in her hand.

G: What are we going to do now?

BETH: We can't let him out, can we?

SAL: It's all gone a bit mad, hasn't it?

SAL starts to giggle and then, gradually, they all do.

LISA: What are you going to do, G?

G: I don't know.

BETH: Hang out for the eighty-five? That was the deal.

G: Do you think?

BETH: Well, we've got a kind of responsibility now, haven't we?

G: I guess so…

MATT: Excuse me? Crazy people? This is Matt McGarry in here, not Jack The fucking Ripper. Let's get this in perspective, shall we? Am I responsible for every woman in this pub being dumped on at some point in their lives? Is that reasonable?

LISA: No, Matt. But, you see, you've become symbolic now. You've got a sort of responsibility too…

BETH: Yeah, it's a kind of a compliment, if you think about it…

G: I don't know what to do. I mean, I don't really care about the other money. I have got the fifty quid back.

BETH: You did have. How much of it have you got left?

G: Well, I've got this ten…

LISA: I've got some change from the wine actually, sorry, I forgot…

BETH: How much?

LISA: (*Counting it out of her pockets.*) …seven fifty.

BETH: Okay…that makes seventeen pounds fifty. What's that off of fifty quid?

SAL: Thirty two pounds fifty.

BETH: Right…the deal was eighty-five, he's paid fifty. So he owes thirty-five anyway. And you need another thirty two pounds fifty to cover your expenses for getting the original fifty, otherwise it's all been a waste of time, hasn't it?

MATT: What?

G: Yeah, but Beth, they're not going to pay it, are they? His mates, I mean…

BETH: Probably not, no. But if we let him out now, he's getting off too lightly, isn't he?

LISA: So…we make him do time.

MATT: *What?*

LISA: Yeah, we just keep him locked up until we've had enough. Till we've drunk the scotch. That way it doesn't look like we've backed down.

G: Like, community service?

LISA: Kind of…

BETH: Thirty-two pounds fifty's worth? What do you think, G? You might as well get value for your money…

G: I guess… I mean, he deserves it, doesn't he? What do you think, Sal?

SAL: I don't care. I don't want to go outside anyway. The place is full of couples.

BETH: We'll have our own party in here then. Okay?

G: Okay.

BETH: Is everybody agreed?

Everyone agrees.

Blackout.

End of Act One.

ACT TWO

The door handles and all around MATT's door is now strewn with tights. There are tights tied to the toilet roll dispenser in the left hand toilet which now, by a series of knots, go all the way over to the other side of the cubicles, keeping the door on top of MATT's cubicle in place. Even so, LISA and SAL are lying on the door. The other women are all sitting around on the toilet floor. DILLY has returned and some of them are drinking whisky, some wine. There is a kind of laid-back late night feel about it. Semi-drunken.

LISA: What do you think about those old songs where people die of broken hearts? Do you think they're true?

BETH: What old songs?

LISA: Old folk songs, you know, where the lovers get split up for some reason, like their parents make them marry someone else or one of them gets killed, and then the other one dies, of a broken heart. *You know…*

The others look blank.

I wonder if people really did? And if they did, why don't they do it any more?

SAL: (*A little drunkenly.*) They probably died of alcoholic poisoning. They just didn't have autopsies in those days.

MATT: (*Desperately.*) I'm going to die of alcohol withdrawal. At least give me a light, girls…come on…

LISA: There's one called 'Anarchie Gordon', right, where he's this girl, Jeannie's lover but he's also a sailor, so whilst he's at sea…

BETH: Who?

LISA: Anarchie Gordon.

BETH: That's a name?

LISA: Yeah. So whilst he's at sea, Jeannie's father tells her she has to marry Lord Sultan and Jeannie says she will but she won't sleep with him…

DILLY: Lord who?

LISA: Sultan. He's this guy with loads of money, right? So on the wedding night, Jeannie's father orders her maids to undress her…

SAL: That's horrible!

LISA: Yeah.…but then Jeannie says she'd rather die than give herself to anyone else but Anarchie…so she does.

DILLY: What?

LISA: Die.

SAL: How?

LISA: I don't know. She just does. And then Anarchie comes home and finds out she's dead and he kisses her corpse and dies as well.

MATT: He kisses her corpse?

LISA: 'He kissed her cold lips
and his heart turned to stone
and he died in the chamber
his true love lay in'

Pause.

BETH: Perhaps she had some sort of a disease…

DILLY: People were always dying in those days…

SAL: Didn't Romeo do that too?

G: He stabbed himself, didn't he?

LISA: No, Juliet stabbed herself. Romeo drank poison.

MATT: Juliet shot herself.

DILLY: Only in the film, you twat.

LISA: So…do you think that could happen nowadays?

BETH: Your wistful tone implies that you think it's a good thing, Lisa…

LISA: Well, I don't know. Do you think that people love each other enough nowadays to die of a broken heart? I mean, to physically die?

SAL: I've had this sort of lump in my stomach all week. It's there at the moment. That's why I can't eat.

BETH: It's a love tumour. Sal's going to *die.*

SAL: It's not funny. I wake up in the morning and it's still there. It feels like I've swallowed a rabbit or something.

G: I know what you mean.

BETH: Oh my God, they're both going to die. I'm afraid I really don't think that Steve or Matt are worth dying over…

DILLY: They're not even worth stepping over…

LISA: There you go, you see. That's what I mean.

BETH: Oh please, Lisa. Do tell us what you mean…

LISA: That love's not the same any more. Maybe. That people don't put their whole selves into it now. Like… what's the first thing that happens after you sleep with somebody?

BETH: You itch.

MATT: They steal your clothes

LISA: You both get nervous, don't you? You act like it's nothing important. You play it cool. Nobody's got the courage to say 'God, yeah, that was great, let's do it forever!' in case that scares the other one off.

SAL: Not always.

LISA: I mean, look at films. In films, a couple get it together and it's all really amazing, isn't it? They both come first time and then they're both in love straight away and they're going to be together for the rest of their lives. But that hasn't happened to us, has it? Real people say, ' look, I've just finished with somebody and I need to sort my head out, okay?' or 'I'll see you around' – if they say anything at all – and, I mean, I just can't see anyone nowadays being *reckless* enough to die of a broken heart, can you?

BETH: You're missing a point, Lisa…

LISA: What's that?

BETH: That all those stories and songs have been written by someone. They're not real. Romeo and Juliet meet at a party and get married the next day, right?…come on, that doesn't happen does it? But Shakespeare *wanted* it to and so did the audience. Everybody *wants* to believe in this amazing kind of love which doesn't actually exist. Somebody made it up.

SAL: You're such a cynic, Beth. Don't you believe in love at all?

BETH: I'm a realist, Sal. You've got to get with it. It's no good waiting around for some guy to shin up your drainpipe and start tossing off poems about you.

LISA: Wouldn't that be romantic though?

BETH: No. You'd think he was a freak. He'd break the drainpipe. Or he'd fall off it and sue you.

SAL: Oh, Come on…

BETH: Romance is for scriptwriters, okay? They have loads of time to think about what lovers *should* say to one another when they first meet or after their first shag, but in real life, you don't know anything and you're probably pissed and it's six o'clock in the morning and all you want to do is get some sleep.

LISA: …I guess in films too, you've only got two hours to make it happen, haven't you? So everything's kind of speeded up, isn't it?

BETH: Exactly. In real life, it takes you six months just to notice someone's there, another few months to talk to them, another few months to sleep with them, a night to fall in love with them…

G: …a minute to fall out of love with them…

DILLY: And ten years wishing you hadn't started in the first place.

They laugh. SAL looks pensive.

SAL: Our grandfather died of a broken heart, though, didn't he, Beth?

BETH: He died of a stroke, Sal.

SAL: Yeah, but, it was six months after Grandma died and there was nothing wrong with him before. Everybody says so. They say he just gave up. That he didn't want to live without her. You know that, Beth. You're just trying to be cool.

BETH: It's different with old people, isn't it?

SAL: Why?

BETH: Because most of them have been together since they were twenty one or something. They don't know how to live on their own. They can't stand the loneliness, so they stop looking after themselves, they stop caring. I suppose you can call it dying of a broken heart if you like.

SAL: What do you call it?

BETH: A cop out.

SAL: If old people can give up and let themselves die, why can't we?

BETH: Why would we? Our generation has moved on, Sal.

SAL: Love is an emotion, not a fashion, Beth.

BETH …we've become emotionally liberated. We've slept with more than one person so we know that there's more than one person out there. We've disproved The myth of the 'other half'. We don't have to give up and die because it doesn't work out with somebody. Just wait a while, and try again.

LISA: I never understood how Heathcliff died.

DILLY: Wasn't he always foaming at the mouth? It might have been rabies…

BETH: I wouldn't die for a man.

MATT: I'd die for a fag…

BETH: Would you, Matt? Can we quote you on that?

LISA: Wouldn't any of you like to be that in love though?

DILLY: No.

G: Matt wouldn't. It's not cool, is it Matt?

MATT: Anything you say, G. You know everything about me.

G: It wouldn't be exciting enough for you. You'd never know what you were missing, would you? There might be someone out there who gives a better blow job, mightn't there? Or Somebody with bigger tits or longer hair…what are you going to do when you've shagged everyone in town, Matt? Move somewhere else, or start at the beginning again?

MATT: (*Getting louder.*) Will you *shut up moaning*? You're doing my head in…

LISA: …the thing is, I mean, to be in love with someone who feels exactly the same as you do, right from the start. And isn't scared to admit it. Wouldn't that be amazing? But it's almost like there's something wrong with being in love. Like it's something to be ashamed of. It's almost considered a weakness…

DILLY: It is. It makes you weak and stupid. All the things you could handle by yourself before, you suddenly need help with. You need him to unblock the kitchen sink when you've done it a million times yourself. All of a sudden, he can't iron the shirt he's had for years…

SAL: It doesn't have to be like that.

BETH: It doesn't, but you have to fight it. I get such a buzz out of watching a man try to fix a puncture for me. I could do it myself easily, but it's so nice not to.

DILLY: Yeah, Beth, but what do you have to give in return? As soon as you let them do things like that, you start giving up your freedom. You start pushing off your self-respect. Till you forget that you're quite capable of being on your own, and you become afraid of it. You've got to be so careful. It's easy to lose your independence, but it's not so easy to get it back. It took me a long time. I mean it.

SAL: But me and Steve weren't like that.

DILLY: Weren't you? You keep mentioning his name, Sal. You can't let go of it, can you? See what I mean? You're scared of being on your own again.

SAL: I'm not scared of it, I just don't want to be. And I don't want to be with anyone else either. I want to be with him. I mean, what is so bad about that?

DILLY: Mainly the fact that he doesn't want to be with you.

SAL: Well, he might change his mind…I mean, maybe he just needs some space, like he said…

DILLY: Oh God, Sal. Get with it. They're not worth it…

SAL: So what are you saying? That we should all live on our own forever? And never fall in love with anyone?

DILLY: Yeah. Live on your own. Keep them at a distance. Don't let them get to you.

SAL: I think that's really sad. You're so bitter, Dill. Maybe you're just scared of being in love again. And maybe that's just as bad.

BETH: Steady on, girls…

SAL: And you…you pretend that nobody gets to you, but it's bullshit, Beth. I don't believe it. You loved Pete, didn't you? You were happy living with him…

BETH: Yeah, I was, Sal. Pete was a special person. But special people don't turn up every day. You've got to be able to tell the difference.

SAL: And you don't think I can? You think you're the only one clever enough to do that. You don't think Steve was special, obviously. Just another one of Sal's little clowns… But maybe you're wrong – maybe he was my other half, maybe that's not a myth at all, maybe there is somebody that's meant for you…

DILLY: Shouldn't you be meant for him back though? I mean, he seems to be coping quite well on his own. Or with Karen.

BETH: (*Hastily.*) Perhaps he was someone special. I'm just saying he's not the only one. There'll be others…

SAL: And I'll get over it…

BETH: Well, I hope you'll get over it, yeah.

SAL: I'm not sure I even want to. I don't know if I want to be like you…or like any of you…

BETH: I'm not asking you to be like me. I just don't want you slitting your wrists on me, okay?

SAL: I'll do it in private then.

BETH: You're drunk, Sal.

SAL: You told me to get drunk. Advice from Big Sister, right?

BETH: Oh, I'm sorry I spoke! I'm sorry I tried to help! Go and stick your head in an oven then, Sal, if you feel you have to. I won't say another word, okay? Because you're obviously the only person who's ever felt like this. And I'm obviously too shallow to understand. I mean – what would I know?

An awkward pause. LISA decides to breech it.

LISA: I read somewhere that in really ancient times, right, all the women used to live in one part of the woods and all the men used to live in another, and that they'd only get together to make babies, basically, which the women would then bring up by themselves, but all together, you know, like a communal thing…

MATT: Sounds like a great idea to me…

LISA: …and you didn't have a husband or anything…I mean, the kids didn't have any particular man for a father…they'd have these sort of festivals where you'd sleep with as many men as you could, just to insure you got pregnant, you know… Like Morrismen.

DILLY: Morrismen?

LISA: Yeah. They used to have May festivals where everyone would go off into the woods and shag and you couldn't tell who the father was if he was a Morrisman because he'd be in disguise. That's where the surname Morrison comes from.

G: So much for your old-fashioned love, Lisa…

LISA: Well, it's a different thing, but I rather like the idea, don't you?

BETH: Of what? Shagging a Morrisman? They're not exactly sex on legs are they? It'd be like shagging a bleeding reindeer – all those bells and sticky outy bits…

LISA: Haven't you ever seen the ones with the blacked up faces? They look like something from Hell. And You can't tell what they really look like at all. I quite like the idea of shagging somebody faceless like that… Down an alleyway, perhaps.

BETH: You're just weird. I suppose you'd like to sleep with a clown too?

LISA: Not as sexy. Interesting though.

DILLY: He could probably show you a trick or two

BETH: He should know how to tumble, shouldn't he?

DILLY: What about in the morning, though? All his make up would have come off. Then what? He could turn out to be about sixty-five and covered in broken veins…

LISA: …or about twelve and covered with acne…

G: Yeah, and think what a state your sheets would be in…

BETH: You sling him out before the morning, don't you?

MATT: Will you lot *listen* to yourselves?

LISA: (*Curiously.*) Has that ever happened to you, Matt?

MATT: What? Have I ever chucked somebody out so I didn't have to see them in the morning? Well, I must have done, I'm the bastard, aren't I?… Did I ever do that to you, G?

LISA: No, I mean, have you ever woken up with a woman who looked completely different to how she did the night before?

MATT: Yeah. Of course I have. Every bloke has.

DILLY: Matt probably can't remember who he was with the night before. It probably was someone different.

LISA: That must be quite bizarre.

MATT: It's scary, but we deal with it. Because we're alright really. We're not monsters. We don't lock people up in toilets on *New Year's Eve* and give them fags without lighters and nothing to drink while we have a fucking Ann Summers party outside…

LISA: …I went to one of those once, it was horrific. They made me kneel down blindfold, while one of them fed me a banana. She really shoved it down my throat too. I was nearly sick.

DILLY: She was obviously getting her own back for something…

LISA: Yeah, but, why me? I haven't eaten a banana since…

BETH: Mmm? but have you…?

LISA: Not in that position.

G: Men look exactly the same in the morning, don't they?

DILLY: That's only because they look so rough to start with.

MATT: I thought you liked a bit of rough, Dill.

DILLY: Who asked you?

MATT: Anyone would think you didn't like men at all, the way you go on…

DILLY: I don't. Much.

MATT: You shag them though, don't you?

DILLY: Everybody slips up.

MATT: And lands on their back, right? Yeah, there are a lot of banana skins in the road, aren't there? Or, then again, maybe you're just full of shit, eh?

BETH: Ooh. Fighting talk from the Musketeer…have you got your sword drawn, D'Artagnan?

DILLY: Me full of shit? That's a laugh. You're so full of shit, it's a wonder you can walk.

MATT: Yeah yeah yeah. Whatever you say, Dilly.

SAL: Who have you been shagging, Dilly?

BETH: Not Portos-because-he-drinks-Port? (*To LISA.*) What's the other one called?

LISA: Arsehole-because-he's-an-Arsehole?

They laugh.

MATT: (*Singing softly.*) I'm Dill the dog…
I'm a dog called Dill…

G: Why are you having a go at her?

MATT: I'll tell you, shall I? Shall I tell them, Dill?
…because I'm getting fucking sick of this. I am fucking sick of sitting in here and listening to all this feminist bullshit. All this *hypocrisy* is making my teeth itch. And I don't like small spaces and I'm starting to sweat and if you don't let me out soon, like, *now*, I think I might just lose my self-control…does anybody catch my drift?…

DILLY looks at her watch.

DILLY: Oh, look, it's nearly midnight! Shall we go outside? Just to sing Auld Lang Syne?

MATT: Hello?

LISA: Good idea. Let's all go…Beth?

BETH: Sure. Come on, Sal…

SAL: I don't know…

BETH: Come on, Misery. You too, G. Lighten up a bit. It is New Year, after all. I'm dying for a piss, anyway.

SAL: (*As they're leaving.*) Oh, I see. It's alright for me to piss in front of him…

BETH laughs. The girls all exit the toilet, leaving MATT alone.

MATT: Oi! Where are you going? Come back here, you bunch of slappers! You can't leave me in here!

MATT rattles the door and bangs the 'roof', all to no avail. He goes down on the floor and sticks his head in the gap between the door and floor and tries to wriggle through. He gets stuck at the ribs, his nose pressed to the floor.

(*Muffled.*) Bloody hell. Okay, count to ten. Deep breaths. We're going to get out of here. Think Steve McQueen.

He retreats, turns around and tries to wriggle through feet first. He sticks at his ribs again. He sighs heavily, retreating into the cubicle.

This is some fucking party, innit? (*Shouts loudly.*) Happy New Year, everyone! Fancy a snog, Mop? Or maybe not. Your hair stinks. You bleach it, don't you? Try washing it mate. Christ – what is that smell? That is not Mop. (*He scrambles around with his hand.*) Urgh! Oh Jesus! I'm going to be sick! ...and they say we're slobs...

Suddenly, a mobile phone starts to ring – it is coming from MATT's jacket, outside his cubicle.

Eh?

MATT's scrambles around and his head appears again. He probes out with the mop to try and pull the jacket to the door.

Come on baby, come to Daddy...

He finally achieves it and takes out the phone. It stops. The sound of 'Auld Lang Syne' filters into the toilet. He is pissed off. He withdraws inside the cubicle again. We hear him ring another number.

Come on Sparky – pick up the phone...pick it up boy, go on...

Sparky doesn't.

You wanker! Yeah, and auld lang syne to you too, mate. What the fuck does that mean, anyway?

MATT retreats and sits back on the toilet.

New Year's bloody eve. Stuck in a girl's bog. What did I do to deserve this? Eh? Fucking women. Fucked up, the lot of them. I don't know why I have anything to do with them. This is it. Me and women are finished. They're mad, vain… unhygenic…extremely uncool and…

The phone rings again (some stupid overture type ring – very uncool) inside the cubicle, MATT breaks off. A pause.

Oh, Hello Mum. Yeah. Happy New Year. You having a good time? Yeah. Great. Yeah. It's kicking in here. Oh, all my mates, you know. Yeah yeah. Yeah, it's a laugh. No, course you're not. What would you be interrupting? (*Laughs nervously.*) Well, you know you come first Mum, eh? I'll kiss her in a minute. (*Slightly hysterically.*) Yeah, she's here, yeah . Yeah – she's having a ball – she's having a pair of them – What? No, just a joke. I'll tell her that, yeah. No, I'm fine, honestly. *Mum…* Look, you have a good time, okay? And I'll see you soon, Alright? Got to go – Goodbye now. Yep. Bye, Mum. Yep. Love you too. Christ almighty. My Mum's having a better time than I am. (*Pause. More dialling.*) Hello? Is that The Crisis Line? Yeah, I just got your number off the back of a toilet door… well, yeah, it is in the ladies, yeah… Okay, so I'm a bloke. Doesn't mean I can't have a crisis, does it? What? Well, as it happens, I'm locked in. The ex locked me in. And her band of psycho mates. It's not funny… Oi! Are you getting paid for this? Is there a bloke there I can talk to? A what? A taxi driver? Well, yeah…I guess he'll do… Alright, mate? Busy night? Yeah, I appreciate that. I'd be calling you myself in a minute, only… oh, she told you. Right. Yeah, I can see how it might seem to be very amusing but it's kind of got beyond that point now, okay? I was just having a drink with the boys, you know, minding my own business when suddenly she goes mad on me – hauls me in here… It could be, mate – who knows? It's always some time of the month, isn't it? They can have premenstrual tension for two to three weeks nowadays, followed by five days of belly aching and then your post-menstrual stress…you never know when it's safe to go round… They should. They should wear badges. You're right. So I slept with someone else, yeah? Right. Big fucking deal. You're absolutely right. I mean, it was obviously over. She knew that. But she wasn't going to make it easy for me, was she? Oh no. She had to make me be the bastard. Tradition? That's an interesting word, mate. Yeah, but is it fair? I mean, do we enjoy this? Am I having the time of my life here? You're right again, mate. I am not.

SAL stumbles back into the toilet. She is weeping silently.

I mean…I didn't want to go off her, did I? It just happens – there's nothing you can do about it. One minute they're all fluffy and cute – or…yes…like Madonna…if you like…then the next minute they've got spots on the end of their nose and a whiny voice that bores the shit out of you. It's fucking tragic, really. You know what I'm saying?

SAL wanders over to the mirrors. She holds her head in her hands.

Right. And, I mean, we had some good times. We had a laugh – but that's not enough, is it? She has to start getting heavy, you know? She starts leaving her clothes in my room and giving her mates my phone number and – well – moving in…absolutely. They're bloody sneaky like that, aren't they? You *have* got to watch them. When you go in your bathroom one day and find ten different types of shampoo in there, it's time to pay attention.

SAL is listening. She looks round at the door, then back at the mirror, she looks at herself hard in the mirror, as if recognising this.

And then I start noticing things, you know? Like how she sniffs all the time and how she swallows tea. You

know what I mean? Well, that too. It's the same thing.
She says something all dog-eyed like 'you don't fancy
me any more, do you, Matt?' and that's it – whack – (*Big
slurp noise, gulp.*) No kidding. The fucking plumbing on
that woman. It's the first thing I'm going to check out in
future. Cup of tea, darling? (*Big slurp noise, gulp.*) No way.
I can see that you know what I'm talking about here.
And now this. God, I mean – this is pathetic, isn't it?
What does she think she's going to get out of this? Fifty
quid, my arse. She's just stretching it out even more, isn't
she? I couldn't have put it better myself. No fucking
pride.

SAL starts to cry again, noisily this time.

Hang on a minute, mate… Who's that?

Silence.

Who is it? G? It's not you, is it? Is it?

SAL: (*Through tears, muffled.*) No…

MATT: Who is it?

Pause.

Dill?

*MATT gets down onto the floor of the toilet, we can see his
head in the gap.*

MATT: Dilly? I know it's you. I can see your boots.

*SAL looks down at DILLY's boots, which she is still wearing,
but says nothing. She is still crying.*

What's the matter with you?…and don't you fucking lay
it on me, either. What with all the crap you've given out
tonight. Cut off my balls with a carving knife, wouldn't
you, Dill-The-Feminist? Dill-The-Dog, more like. Got
nothing else to say? What's up – swallowed your tail? I
hope you've noticed that I haven't dropped you in it. You
want to check you've got both earrings in next time you
leave somebody's bedroom, Dilly.

Pause. More crying.

What? Oh yeah, sorry mate, I'm going to have to go.
Eh? No, it's the other one. Yeah, thanks, I need it. Yeah.
Will do. Car sixty-five, yeah? Ask for Bill? Definitely.
Well, if I don't, have a good night anyway. You too. It's
been nice talking to you. We must have a pint sometime.
Sure. Okay. Bye. (*To 'Dill' again.*) Oh stop it, will you?
What's the matter? Didn't get a midnight snog? It's not
too late, darling – just open the door – I'm all puckered
up. It might be quite a wise move anyway, if you don't
want to end up in the next cubicle. Cause they wouldn't
be that impressed really, would they? If they knew. Not
exactly a girl's best friend, are you? And I don't know if
I can keep my mouth shut much longer. What have I got
to lose? I've been sentenced already, haven't I? I'm a
nasty, filthy man. I was born a nasty, filthy man. It's not
even my fault really, is it? What's your excuse? Dill?
(*Pause.*) Talk to me, will you? Look, there's no need for
us to fall out, is there? I mean, once this has all blown
over, maybe we could go out for a drink or something,
yeah? How about it? I thought we were pretty good
together, didn't you? Dilly? Why don't you let me out
now, before they all come back and we won't say a word,
okay? Come on, Dill.

Pause.

SAL: I'm not Dill.

Silence.

MATT: Oh.

Pause and then MATT says, hopefully.

There's no chance of you being a normal person is
there?

SAL: It's Sal.

MATT: Oh.

SAL: It was Dilly. Who you slept with.

Silence.

MATT: Don't tell G, Sal. She'll go ballistic. You're a mate of Dill's, aren't you?

SAL: Not any more.

MATT: Oh, come on. You know how things happen. It's no big deal. You'll make a big deal out of it if you tell G…

SAL: No big deal?

MATT: If it wasn't Dill, it would've been someone else. It just happened to be Dill. It's better left, isn't it?

SAL: Was Dill your 'back-up'?

MATT: Look, I'm sorry about that, Sal…

SAL: Steve's snogging his 'back-up' right now. Out there. They didn't even bother doing Auld Lang Syne. Just went straight into the snog.

MATT: It doesn't mean anything, Sal. It's just New Year, isn't it?

SAL: (*Shouting.*) It means something to me! (*SAL kicks MATT's door violently.*)

MATT: (*Shaken.*) Okay. Alright. Calm down.

SAL: He didn't even see me…

It goes very quiet. SAL goes back to the mirror. She fumbles in BETH's bag until she finds the lipstick. Tries to put some on but her hands are shaking uncontrollably. MATT is straining to see her from under the door. She gives up on her face and 'slashes her wrists' with the lipstick, leaving bright red marks, then sinks to the floor with her head in her hands, crying again. MATT is not sure what he has seen.

MATT: Sal?

Silence.

Sal? What have you done? You haven't done anything stupid, have you?

Still silence. MATT rattles the door with rising panic.

Sal? Come on. Speak to me...

SAL lifts her head up, and turns to MATT. He sees her wrists.

SAL: Speak to you? Why would I want to speak to you?

MATT: Jesus Christ! What have you done?

SAL: What?

MATT: Sal, sweetheart. Come over here. We need to sort you out. Come on.

SAL looks at her wrists and realises.

SAL: It's only lipstick, Matt.

MATT breathes a sigh of relief.

MATT: Thank Christ for that.

SAL: Yeah, like you care.

MATT: You think I've never been there, don't you? You think nobody's ever broken my heart?

SAL: Have you got a heart?

MATT: Vanessa Bird.

SAL: Who?

MATT: She broke my heart. First time. I was only seventeen. I locked myself in my room and took a whole jar of Multivitamins. I thought I would die.

SAL: What happened?

MATT: Well I lived, didn't I? (*Laughs.*) I've never felt so fucking healthy in my life.

SAL: No, I mean, what happened with Vanessa Bird?

MATT: She went off with someone else. They always do, Sal. People move on.

SAL: But what's the point of starting something with someone if you know it's just going to end?

MATT: What's the point of getting up in the morning when you know you're going to end up back in bed? You've got to think of each one as another adventure, that's all. Enjoy it while you can. Look back at the snapshots.

SAL: Steve was a bit more than a fucking holiday snap! Why can't anybody understand that?

G starts coming into the toilet at this point. She hears them talking and stops, listens.

MATT: You've got to toughen up a bit if you want to survive, okay? You feel like shit now, but, give it a couple of weeks and you won't feel so bad. You'll just feel angry and you'll start hating him. Like G hates me…

SAL: I won't…

MATT: You will, right. And then you'll get all bitter and twisted for a while and you'll say all men are arseholes…till one night you're a bit lonely and you meet somebody who doesn't seem like *such* an arsehole and you'll sleep with him for the hell of it and it'll be nice, you know, you'll be surprised. And he won't be able to hurt you like Steve has because you won't let him. You'll be in control, Sal, because you'll accept things for what they are. That's what you've got to do if you want to grow old.

SAL: Oh, you're so mature, aren't you? You sound just like Beth.

MATT: Yeah, well. Beth's got it sorted, hasn't she?

SAL: Has she? Have you? What about you and Dill?

MATT: Me and Dill both know the score.

The others come in behind G. She gestures to them to be quiet.

SAL: Do you? I'm confused, Matt. I mean, If you and Dill are both so tough and uninvolved and *heartless* – if you're both so cool about it and *unattached*, then why did Dilly help G lock you up in the toilet and why have you been bitching at each other all night?

MATT: Oh, that just happens sometimes, doesn't it…you know…after a one-night-stand…

SAL: Does it? Why should it? Isn't it actually because you like one another and you're pretending not to? Because you won't allow yourselves to? And isn't that *really* stupid? Isn't that the *really stupidest* way to be? Do you really think I want to be like that? Do you really think I want to be like *you*? The trouble is with all of this is that nobody tells one another the truth. Why not? What is everyone so afraid of?

MATT: Seems to me that you're the one who's afraid of the truth, Sal.

G turns around and stares at DILL, who is just behind her. DILL turns around to go, but BETH and LISA are inadvertently blocking her way. G takes DILL by the hand and skips her into the room. She sings dangerously.

G: 'Who's afraid of the big bad truth, the big bad truth, the big bad truth?'

SAL: (*Jumping up in surprise.*) G? …you're back…

G: Yes. Have we missed anything?

SAL: No…I was just…we were just…

G: Yes, I heard. Are you playing the truth game? Great. We'll all play. Do you want to play, Dill? I haven't played it for years. How does it start again? Somebody asks a question and everyone has to answer it truthfully.

That's it isn't it? Like, do you smell your finger after you scratch your bum? Or…have you ever slept with your best friend's boyfriend?… Let's start with that one, shall we? Me first. No I haven't. Who's next then? Oh, it must be you, Dill.

DILLY: Thanks a lot, Matt.

G: Oh my God, look. She's even thanking him for it. Well I guess that answers that question.

DILLY: Hang on a second, G…

G pushes DILL so that she staggers back into SAL's toilet. SAL scrambles out of the way and up onto the top of MATT's cubicle.

G: For what? Dear life?

G bangs on MATT's door.

G: Hey, lover boy, how are you doing in there? I bet you've never had such a good night, have you? You must be laughing your fucking head off.

MATT: Yeah. Ha ha ha. Bonk.

G: (*Turning to DILLY.*) You always said he was *such* a prick, Dill. I didn't think you meant it literally.

DILLY: He is a prick, G. Let me explain…

G: I just don't believe this. How could you do this? It was your earring, then?

DILLY: (*Sighing.*) Yeah, G. It was my earring.

G: Do you want it back?

DILLY: What?

G: I've still got it, if you do…

DILLY: G, it's a fucking earring. Forget the earring…

G: Oh, but it's really nice, Dill. I've never seen you wear it before. Was it new?

DILLY: It's a lousy earring. Keep it, G. I'll even give you the other one. Will you just let me explain how it happened...?

G: Yeah, why don't you?

DILLY: You were away, right? Back at your parents? Everyone from college had gone away and I was kind of lonely... I mean, it was Christmas...

G: Oh! It was Christmas! Help yourself to the fucking cake!

DILLY: ...I went out looking for someone to drink with and I came across Matt and he said that you and him were finished...

G: Nice of him to tell me!

DILLY: Exactly. *Exactly.* You see?

G: No, I don't see. I would see if you had run back home and rung me to see if I was okay...

DILLY: Oh no, hold on a minute, G. How many times have you rung me lately – to see if *I* was okay?

G: What?

DILLY: Because I wasn't okay, as it happens. I've had quite a lousy time of it lately, if you're interested. And Matt, believe it or not, actually did ask me how I was and actually listened to the answer.

G: Oh God, that's the oldest trick in the book – you fell for that?

DILLY: Look, we got drunk and it happened. I'm sorry. These things happen.

G: Do these things happen twice?

DILLY: Eh?

G: Matt said it happened twice, didn't he? Didn't he say that, Sal? Do you remember him saying that, anyone?

Silence.

Didn't you say that, Matt?

MATT: Are you talking to me?

DILLY: Alright. I slept with him twice. Then you came back and I found out that he'd lied and I realised I'd been fucked over too, and that was that, okay? He lied to me too. He's such a nice guy, isn't he? And now he thought he'd tell everyone. Which is so nice, isn't it? I mean, why keep his mouth shut when he could hurt you even more? Why not make me out to be a cow…?

G: *Make you out* to be a cow? Are you having a laugh, Dill?

DILLY: Come on, who are you going to believe? Me or Matt? Me or The Shagaround?

G: Who are you calling a Shagaround?

BETH: Look, shall we just…I mean, shall we just call this off now? Let's all go back outside and have a beer, eh? It smells of feet in here anyway…

G: Keep out of it, Beth.

BETH: Come on, Sal. Let's get out of here.

SAL: I can't, Beth.

BETH: What do you mean, you can't? You can't what?

SAL: I can't go out there again. I can't bear it.

BETH: We'll go somewhere else then.

SAL: There isn't anywhere to go, is there?

BETH: Sure there is. Everywhere's open till one. And there's some parties after. Come on…

SAL: I mean that everywhere's the same. There's nowhere to go.

BETH: Jesus, Sal. Buck yourself up, will you? We'll spit in his eye as we leave, okay?

SAL: It isn't just Steve. It's everyone. Everyone's the same and it's all so…worthless…

BETH: Cheers, kid. And there, I thought you liked me…

SAL: Look at Dilly – fucking up her best mate for someone she says is a prick – it wouldn't be so bad if she admitted that she liked him – at least then there'd be some point in it…

BETH: Look, this is their argument, Sal. It doesn't involve us any more…

LISA: Everyone's not the same, Sal…

BETH: Course they're not.

SAL: I just think she could at least admit it

BETH: Dill? Will you confess to liking Matt? Can we get this all over with?

DILLY: Confess what? To liking that piece of shit?

G: What's going on now? Dilly slept with my boyfriend and it's alright as long as she liked him? Do I get a say in this? She had no fucking right to like him! Even if she believed that we'd split up, she still knew it would upset me. You're supposed to be my friend, Dilly. I mean, *did* you always fancy him, or what?

DILLY: No, G. I never fancied him.

G: So he raped you. Is that it? And then you went round and he raped you again?

BETH: Cut it out now, come on. This is getting ugly.

G: Will you shut up, Beth? Did he rape you, Dill?

MATT: I didn't fucking rape anybody!

DILLY: G, you're getting hysterical. We're all a bit pissed, right? Maybe we should talk about this tomorrow.

MATT: I'm not sitting in here till tomorrow…

DILLY: (*Turning to the door.*) We'll decide what you do, arsehole. Personally, I think we should leave you in there till the cleaner finds you…

LISA: Well I think we should let him out and go outside. I think Beth's right. This hasn't got anything to do with us any more. The joke's over, isn't it?

G: (*Turning on her.*) This is no fucking joke, Lisa.

LISA: It isn't now, I know. It's getting too heavy for me. Let's go to another pub or something.

BETH: I'm with you.

G: So you're just going to cop out, are you? Thanks for your support, girls.

BETH: Look, I'm all for a bit of female solidarity, G, but this is just turning into a scrap between you and Dill…

DILLY: And whose fault is that? Don't you see what he's done? This was never about who he'd slept with. It's not even relevant except that it makes him even more of a shit than he was anyway because he lied to me as well. How do you think I feel?

G: You? We're supposed to care?

DILLY: You're playing right into his hands if you let him get away with it now. Not only has he crapped on both of us, but he's made us crap on one another too.

G: Crap on one another? When have I ever crapped on you?

DILLY: You're crapping on me now, by not even listening to me…

G: Listen to you? God, haven't we been listening to you all night? Going on about how much you hate men – Having the nerve to party along in here and pretend that you're one of us…

DILLY: One of what? The New Amazonians? Who'd be in here now if there was anyone worth shagging outside? Would *you* have come in here with me if you were still with Matt? Or Sal? If Steve hadn't dumped her? You'd be lucky if she'd have popped in for a piss...

BETH: Leave Sal out of it.

DILLY: Oh, sorry, Beth. It's so touching the way you care about Sal. It's nice to see you together again, because it's been a while, hasn't it? I mean – how many times did Sal call you out to play when she was tucked up with Steve, eh?

LISA: Oh, shut up, Dill. We're here to help one another out, aren't we?

DILLY: Are you? Or are you all just huddling up together and slagging off men and waiting till the next one comes along so you can have a real social life again?

BETH: Speak for yourself.

DILLY: You know, as soon as G found that earring, I was her best mate again. She was on the blower before she'd kicked Matt out the door. She probably had to look up my phone-number, she hadn't used it for so long.

G: What are you saying?

DILLY: I'm saying, make up your mind who's side you're on. You know he's a liar – do you want it spelt out for you in fucking neon? Why shouldn't he lie to me? I mean, I did you a favour really, didn't I? You could have gone on with this twat for years. At least now you know what he really thinks of you.

G smacks DILLY round the face, quite suddenly. DILL staggers back. BETH takes hold of G, but she shakes her off. She stands back, however.

Did that make you feel better?

G: (*A little stunned.*) I thought it was worth a try.

DILLY: You should have hit him. In there.

G: You were nearer.

DILLY: Can we talk about this now, please?

    Pause.

G: Is there any Scotch left?

DILLY: What?

BETH: Hooray, at last. Somebody asked a sensible question. Let's down the Scotch and piss off. Agreed?

LISA: Agreed.

G: What about you, Dill? Do you want to piss off?

DILLY: Are you telling me to?

G: I was asking you a question.

DILLY: I think we should leave, yeah.

G: What about Matt?

DILLY: Oh, fuck Matt.

G: After you…

    BETH picks up the Scotch bottle hastily and hands it to G.

BETH: You get first blast, okay?

    G, slowly and slightly deliriously takes a swig from the bottle and then lowers herself to the floor and leans down to the bottom of MATT's cubicle door. She puts her face into the gap.

G: Would you like some whisky, Matt?

MATT: What?

G: And a light? Would you?

MATT: Yeah, this is a trick, right? You've pissed in it, ha ha.

G: No. It's just that things have changed a bit, haven't they? I feel a bit mean now, leaving you without anything like this. And on New Year's Eve too. I know what a slag Dill can be. You should have told me it was her. It would have made sense.

DILLY: Oh, please…

G: So, anyway…it looks like we're going on somewhere else…

MATT: So, let me out! What are you, crazy? You can't go off and leave me in here…

G: Oh, someone will find you soon enough. Plenty of people come in here to puke this time of night. Just take the scotch and have a smoke until we're all gone and somebody else comes in…

MATT: Jesus Christ…

G: (*Whispering.*) I'll tell your mates they can come and rescue you, okay? (*Normal voice.*) So what? Do you want a light or don't you?

DILLY: Just leave him there, G. He doesn't deserve it. What are you doing that for?

G: (*Lightly.*) Shut it, Dill. He was my boyfriend, okay?

She holds the lighter into the gap. MATT's head gradually appears. He can't quite reach it.

MATT: Pass it in, I can't reach that.

G bends right down to face him. She puts the lighter further in. She has turned it up to full blast, so that when she lights it a high flame belts up which she flicks into his face. He rolls back, swearing.

G: Happy New Year, arsehole!

MATT: You've burnt my face, you stupid bitch. I can't see!

DILLY: G? What have you done? Are you alright, Matt?

G: (*Sarcastically.*) Are you alright, Matt? Darling? Are you okay?

She flicks the lighter towards DILLY's hair. DILLY cuffs her aside.

LISA: You're going too far, G.

MATT: I can't fucking see, man. You've blinded me. I'm not kidding

G: Am I going too far, Dilly?

BETH: (*Impatiently.*) You'll be going to Holloway if we don't calm this thing down. Christ Almighty. What did you do that for? What's the matter, Matt?

MATT: I'm burnt. It feels bad, Beth. I need cold water, don't I?

G: So, stick your head down the toilet, stupid!

BETH: Okay, I've had enough of this.

G: He's having you on, Beth. There's nothing wrong with him.

BETH: Look, I've been working all week in fucking Casualty, I don't need it.

G: So fuck off then. Go outside. Go to another pub. Who's asking you to stay?

MATT: I am! Beth? You're a nurse, right? You can't just leave me. I'm serious. Lisa? You're not a psycho are you?

LISA: Let's open the door, for God's sake. This has got out of hand.

SAL: Let him out, Beth.

BETH goes towards the tights fastening the door. She tries to untie them, which is difficult. G pulls her away. BETH is very impatient now. She goes to her bag and takes out the Swiss army knife, brandishes it at G.

BETH: Get out of the way, okay? I've had it with you now.

Meanwhile, SAL has been scrambling about on the top of the door to see what is going on. She decides to get off it at this point and starts to climb down.

G: I'm telling you, there's nothing wrong with him. He's winding you up.

BETH: We'll see, won't we?

She cuts the tights on the door and, as she does, MATT (who is fine), whacks the door open from the inside so that it swings open with phenomenal force and slams straight into SAL, who has got so far as to be standing behind it. She is thrown back violently and falls backwards onto the first cubicle toilet hitting her head with a crack.

MATT: (*Triumphantly.*) Ta da! Had you going, hey? Cheers, Beth! My only friend!

BETH: (*Still holding the knife out.*) You little fucker!

MATT: What are you going to do with that? Pick my hooves?

He plucks the knife out of her hand and tutts condescendingly.

Thanks for an interesting evening, girls, but I think it's time I was on my way...

G: Do you?

G knees him in the groin before he can go anywhere. He staggers forward, in pain.

MATT: Definitely

He moves towards the exit door but DILLY has got there first and is barring it.

DILLY: Not so fast, D'Artagnan. You're going to tell G the truth first, aren't you?

MATT: What?

DILLY: That you lied to me.

MATT: Yes, G, I lied to Dilly, okay?

DILLY: Why did you do that, Matt?

MATT: Why did you believe me?

BETH rolls her eyes, she thinks this is stupid.

BETH: Come on, Sal. We're out of here. (*She walks over to collect her bag.*)

DILLY: You're such a shit, aren't you?

MATT: Oh just get over it Dill, and get out of the way.

BETH: Sal?

LISA: Let him go, Dill.

DILLY: Promise me you'll never lie to a woman again and I'll let you go.

MATT: Whatever you say.

DILL doesn't move. Meanwhile, BETH has discovered SAL. She stands at the entrance to the cubicle, stunned. LISA notices.

LISA: What's the matter, Beth?

BETH: Oh, Jesus, Lisa.

LISA goes over to BETH, while BETH enters the cubicle. She kneels by SAL.

Sal?

LISA: Shit. What's happened?

BETH: She must have been hit by the door...

LISA: Is she unconscious or what?

G looks over to LISA and SAL. MATT tries to push past DILLY but she grabs his arm. They are close together – a possibly sexual moment.

G: What's the matter?

BETH: Help me get her out of here.

DILLY notices the others.

DILLY: What's going on?

G takes SAL's legs, struggling.

BETH: Take her legs, Matt. Go and ring an ambulance, Lisa.

LISA: An ambulance?

BETH: Yes. Now!

LISA: Has anyone got any change?

BETH: What???

MATT: Here, Lisa… (*MATT gives LISA, who is still looking bewildered, his phone.*)

LISA: Oh God…

They all help to drag SAL out of the cubicle except for LISA who looks at the phone with panic.

DILL: What's the matter with her?

LISA: Do you have to put the code in, Matt?

MATT: How should I know?

BETH: Are you some sort of fucking idiot? Dial 999, for Christ's sake!

LISA: I'm sorry…

She dials. BETH rolls SAL into the recovery position and looks around frantically.

BETH: Get me some paper towels. Quickly!

G does so. BETH presses a wedge on to SAL's head, where she is bleeding.

LISA: Come on…come on…

MATT: Is she alright?

BETH: What does it fucking look like?

MATT: Don't bite *my* head off.

BETH: I'll bite more than your fucking head off if anything happens to her!

LISA: Hello? Hello? Yes please. I want an ambulance. Really quickly...

G: What's going to happen to her, Beth?

LISA: What? *My* name? Lisa? Is that what you mean? Or hers? Her name's Sal. She's hit her head on the toilet and she's bleeding and everything- she looks terrible – please...

DILLY: Can't we do anything?

BETH: Haven't you done enough?

DILLY: Who? Me?

BETH: All of you!

MATT: What have I done?

BETH: Look at her! This is what you've done!

LISA: What? Oh. Yes. We're in The Green Man. The pub.

Oh God, I don't know – (*desperately, to others.*) – what street are we in?

BETH: For fuck's sake... (*She grabs LISA roughly, snatching the phone and giving her the towels to hold to SAL's head.*) We're in The Green Man on the corner of Dunbar Road. The patient's unconscious. Yes, I'm a nurse, I'm looking after her – just get here quickly – *please...* (*She throws the phone on the floor and returns to SAL.*)

MATT: Should I go and wait for them, Beth?

BETH: Yes. And tell that shit, Steve, to get himself in here.

MATT: Steve?

BETH: Yes! Steve! (*She glares at him and he leaves hurriedly.*)

G: It's my fault, isn't it, Beth?

BETH: Oh Jesus. Just shut up, will you?

G: (*Starting to cry.*) I never meant anyone to get hurt…

BETH: Nobody ever does, do they? But somebody always
does get hurt. And it's never the ones who deserve it
either, is it? (*To herself.*) God – what was this all for?

G: I'm so sorry…

BETH: Why did I make her come out? Why didn't I just
leave her alone?

LISA: She'll be alright, Beth.

BETH: Will she? You're qualified to say that are you?

DILLY: Try and keep calm.

BETH: Try and fuck off!

G: Beth? Is she going to be alright?

BETH: Is she? Does she want to be? Look at her. She's
smiling. Do you see that? She couldn't give a shit. I'm
the only one who gives a shit. Not about her and Steve,
or you and Matt, but just about her. Because *I love her.*
And that's not enough.

DILLY: She knows you love her, Beth…

BETH: But it's not enough, is it? None of you are enough to
one another and that's the fucking tragedy. I've known
Sal all my life and yet that beardy little twat outside has
got closer to her heart in three months than I ever could.
Girl power – Jesus – what utter bullshit that is.

G: That's not fair, Beth.

BETH: No, it's not fair. It's not bloody fair at all. Sex always
comes first, over everything to you, but you don't know
how to love. You expect too much…you want so much
more than there is. And then you all get fucked up.

LISA: Sal will be okay, Beth.

BETH: Yeah, she will be. Because I'm not having her cop out on it.

MATT returns.

Why aren't you outside?

MATT: Dave's gone out there. It's alright.

BETH: Where's Steve?

MATT: He's not here, Beth. He's gone home.

BETH: What?

MATT: He left straight after midnight. With Karen. Sparky saw him.

BETH looks nonplussed for a moment.

I'll go and wait with Dave.

BETH: No. No. You're not going anywhere.

MATT: Eh?

BETH: If I can't have Steve, you'll have to do.

MATT: Do what?

BETH: (*To SAL.*) Sally? Look… Steve's here. He's come to see you.

MATT: What?

BETH gestures for MATT to take SAL's hand. He hesitates.

BETH: (*Hiss-whispered.*) I want to hear you lie, okay? I've heard you're good at it.

MATT: I can't, Beth…I don't sound anything like Steve…

BETH: Look, she probably can't even hear you, but it's worth a try.

MATT: (*Sarcastically.*) Is it alright with you, Dill? Do you mind?

BETH: We're not fucking around now, Matt. You do what I say, okay? Get on with it. (*She pulls his arm fiercely, so that he is kneeling next to SAL.*)

He takes her hand reluctantly.

Don't you want to talk to Steve, Sal? He's says he's really sorry. Didn't you say that, Steve?

MATT hesitates.

Didn't you say that, *Steve?*

MATT: Yeah.

BETH: He says he really loves you. Don't you, Steve?

MATT: Yeah.

Pause. BETH nudges him sharply.

(*Unconvincingly.*) I love you. Sal.

BETH: (*Hissing.*) Kiss her.

MATT: What? No!

BETH: Do it! (*She grabs him and pulls him closer.*)

He bends over her and kisses her.

Everything's going to be alright, see?

MATT: Her lips are really cold, Beth.

BETH feels her pulse, she is getting panicky. They all are.

BETH: Wake up, Sally. Mum's made us *special* breakfast.

LISA: Come on, Sal.

BETH: Then she's going to take us to the zoo. You like the zoo, don't you? (*She chokes up.*)

G: (*To MATT.*) Say something else, Matt

MATT: Like what? I don't know what to say…

DILLY: Oh, come on! What do you normally say?

LISA: Please Matt. Just try.

MATT: Sal? Hey, Sal? It's me. It's Steve…

The others gesture him to carry on, do more.

…You look nice…

They groan – MATT looks desperate.

I like your boots…

BETH: Oh Christ, she's stopped breathing.

BETH feels for a pulse in SAL's neck.

G: (*Pleading.*) Matt…

MATT: *What?*

G: This is for *real…*

BETH flips SAL onto her back and starts to resuscitate. MATT is very scared. ·

MATT: Oh shit…shit! (*He changes gear. Looking at G.*) Look, Sal. I'm really sorry, okay? You know how much I care about you, don't you? Eh? We were made for each other, weren't we? The old team? You and Me. We can sort this out, can't we? Course we can. Come on, Girl.

G turns away, in tears. This is what she'd like to hear. SAL breaks out of the huddle and gets up, without the others responding. They remain grouped around her imaginary body.

SAL: I can hear his voice. It's very small and in the distance, but I hear it and nothing else. And I'm seeping into the floor, I'm being soaked into the earth and getting covered up with snow, and it's heavy like a blanket…or a huge soft wedding dress, or like piles of those crisp, clean sheets you get on hospital beds. It's nice and I feel…safe.

MATT: Karen doesn't mean anything, see? She's history, Sal. It was just a stupid thing, right? I was crazy. But it's all over now. It's you I want. Eh? You and me, eh Sal?

DILL drops her head. She has heard him say this before.

SAL: I want to fall asleep forever. I want to live inside this dream – it's like being underwater – and all I can hear is him – and the grinding of the fishes' teeth…it's peaceful and the pain has gone…

MATT: Just you, Sal. Cause we love each other, don't we, eh? And we're gonna be together forever now, okay? We're going to be all old and wrinkly together and have kids and dogs and all that stuff, aren't we? And rabbits and… (*Desperately.*) …Rabbits… Oh, fucking hell… Rabbits and a garden and our own Christmas tree and… (*He starts to cry.*)

SAL: …and his voice… I heard his voice. I could hardly hear the words but I knew that he was there. And now that I'm in this dream, I can be beautiful again, I can be still and white like a statue and I can hear him and…

MATT: Come back to me, Sal.

BETH drops her head.

SAL: …in this dream I can make him say anything.

Fade to blackout.